WVL 1

KT-514-564

Am I Depressed and What Can I Do About It?

A CBT self-help guide for teenagers experiencing low mood and depression

Shirley Reynolds
and
Monika Parkinson

ROBINSON

ROBINSON

First published in Great Britain in 2015 by Robinson

Important note
This book is not intended as a substitute for medical advice or
treatment. Any person with a condition requiring medical attention
should consult a qualified medical practitioner or suitable therapist.

A CIP catalogue record for this book
is available from the British Library.

ISBN 978-1-47211-453-2 (paperback)
ISBN: 978-1-47211-456-3 (ebook)

Typeset in Gentium by Initial Typesetting Services, Edinburgh
Printed and bound in Great Britain by CPI Group (UK) Ltd, Croydon CR0 4YY

Papers used by Robinson are from well-managed forests and
other responsible sources

MIX
Paper from
responsible sources
FSC® C104740

Robinson
is an imprint of
Constable & Robinson Ltd
Carmelite House
50 Victoria Embankment
London EC4Y 0DZ

An Hachette UK Company
www.hachette.co.uk

www.littlebrown.co.uk

Acknowledgements

Using CBT (Cognitive Behaviour Therapy) to tackle depression and low mood is all about collaboration and partnership. This book has been written with that backdrop. We have been so lucky to be able to collaborate with many inspirational, generous and compassionate people.

In a book like this, which is not written for an academic audience, it is not appropriate to exhaustively cite every influence. We are not even sure we are consciously aware of each and every influence – we have absorbed so much from so many that it becomes impossible to know what idea, what thought, or what insight comes from whom. CBT draws on many different ideas in psychology, it tries to help us make sense of the complex humans that we are, and to find solutions to the problems we face in life. As an academic subject in psychology it is fascinating and tantalizing. CBT has impacted on and inspired the whole field of psychotherapy by putting itself on the line, welcoming critical, high-quality research, and continually developing, improving and innovating.

However, CBT really only comes alive when it is put into action. And, as ever, it is people, always people, who bring it to life.

The first people we need to thank are the many individuals with whom we have worked clinically over many years. They have generously and bravely allowed us to share a part of their lives, to work with them and to learn from their experiences. We hope this book will help others, whom we will never meet, to share in some of that background and learning. We now have pretty good evidence that using CBT techniques, as self-help, can reduce the symptoms of low mood and depression. We hope that his book, written specifically for young people who feel low and sad, will be useful to them.

We have many dear colleagues to thank. Paul Gilbert is a psychological tour de force. His ideas about the critical role of self-compassion have influenced so many of us, in so many ways, large and small. In his curiosity, openness to experience, kindness and tolerance he also personifies the theories he developed. Colleagues at the Sheffield MRC/ESRC Social and Applied Psychology Unit were staunchly out at the front of scientific research into psychotherapy, looking at what it was and how it worked at a time when psychotherapy was generally thought of as an indulgence rather than the essential component of effective healthcare it is today. The late Malcolm Adams was an early, wise and supportive mentor. Malcolm always promoted the model of the scientist practitioner. For him this was not a soundbite – he truly valued the importance of rigorously testing our ideas and theories in real life, with real problems and with real people.

Our colleagues at the University of Reading, at the Charlie Waller Institute, and the Winnicott Research Unit have created a fantastic, stimulating and enjoyable working environment. The School of Psychology and Clinical Language Sciences has encouraged us to look around at the many links between CBT and the rest of academic psychology. It is through exploiting links with the science of psychology and neuroscience, and continuing to develop its basic science, that CBT will continue to flourish.

We enjoy a very close relationship with our NHS colleagues. Despite the real and unrelenting pressures on services, the financial cutbacks, and the rising demand for their services for children, young people and families, our friends working in the NHS continue to provide their very best, to many, at all times. The NHS is an amazing organization, the best in the world. We, and so many millions of other people, are in its debt.

Several of our colleagues provided direct help in the preparation of this book. Elisabeth Norton helped us locate and evaluate many of the Internet-based resources. Several teenagers have given us very helpful, and very honest, feedback on earlier drafts. Dr Laura Pass and Dr Lucy Willetts gave us hugely useful feedback, and drew on their own experience of working clinically with young people and their families, and shared some of their own materials. The success of the *Overcoming Your Child's Fears and Worries* self-help book for parents, written by Dr Lucy Willetts and Dr Cathy Creswell, and proven subsequently to be clinically effective, played an important part in inspiring this book. Our appreciation also goes to Andrew McAleer and Fritha Saunders of Constable and Robinson. Charlie Waller Memorial Trust provided financial and moral support to Shirley Reynolds.

The Trust works to raise awareness of depression and fights stigma. This book is written with those same aims and values.

Finally, we would like to thank our wonderful families for their never-ending support, encouragement, inspiration and understanding.

Follow the Charlie Waller Institute on Twitter @ charliewallerin. Follow Shirley @sci_pract.

Contents

Part 1
Is this book for me?

1 What is depression and what can be done about it?   3

2 Goals   31

Part 2
Looking after yourself

3 Dealing with difficult thoughts and unhelpful
  or risky behaviours   45

4 Looking after yourself – the basics   67

Part 3
Getting started

5 Why me?   107

6 The CBT idea   124

7 I want to make more sense of my depression   135

8 Feeling and doing   151

9 Thoughts on trial   188

10 Testing things out – getting the facts   227

11 Solving problems   247

Part 4
Other things to try

12 Additional tools   267

Part 5
Keeping it going

13 Planning for the future and finding more help   297

Appendix 1: Summary of useful places to find out
more info and help   311

Appendix 2: How to find a therapist   319

Appendix 3: Quick view of the book chapters and topics   329

Appendix 4: Extra copies of worksheets   335

Index   361

Part 1

Is this book for me?

1

What is depression and what can be done about it?

Anyone can get depressed and many teenagers will experience depression. Having depression does not mean there is something wrong with you or that you are weak in any way. Millions of people have been depressed at some time in the past or have depression at this very moment. These people can be found in every country in the world and it does not matter where they come from, who they are, or how old they are. Depression really can happen to anyone.

You may be wondering, 'am I depressed?' In this chapter we are going to explain what is meant by depression and help you to work out whether what you are feeling fits with this description. This book introduces three young people who each have depression and gives details about their feelings, symptoms and the ways they have coped. The chapters following this will suggest a number of strategies or tools to combat depression. Most of the strategies are based on years of scientific research, which shows that they are good at helping people with depression. There are also some additional strategies towards the end of the book, which have been shown to help some people feel better.

The book also highlights other places where you can get more information and help. Having depression can feel extremely lonely and painful. You do not need to suffer alone and the fact that you have picked up this book is a fantastic start to doing something about it. If you have had enough of feeling bad and you are ready to make some changes in order to feel better, then please read on.

Along with this book there is also another book available for parents and carers to read. The book helps parents and other adults to better understand what depression is and how it may be affecting a young person. The same teenagers that are introduced in this book also appear in the parent book, along with their parents. It also contains strategies for parents to use to help their teenager feel better. If you think this is something that could be useful then let your parents know about the accompanying book: *Teenage Depression – A CBT Guide for Parents*.

Am I depressed?

Perhaps someone has given this book to you to read or maybe you found it somewhere yourself. But is this book right for you?

If you have been feeling sad, low, down, blue, uninterested in anything, in a dark place, fed up, down in the dumps, irritable or annoyed, snappy, grumpy, worthless, like everything is too much effort or just simply depressed, then chances are that this is the right book for you.

We want to remind you that you are not alone. It might seem like everyone else in your age group is getting on with things, enjoying themselves without a care in the world and no one else feels the way you do. But the fact is there are many other teenagers who feel this way too:

Did you know that at any point in time, for every one hundred teenagers about five to six of them will be feeling low or depressed for a large part of the time? (Actually, it's probably many more than this but it's impossible to know about everyone.)

This probably means some people at your school or even in your class will also be feeling this way and maybe you didn't even think they had problems.

Sometimes knowing that others feel this way too helps, but some people say that it really doesn't make a big difference because it still feels awful for them.

What is depression?

So what do people mean when they talk about feeling low or having depression?

We all feel sad or low from time to time, it's natural. If we didn't then we wouldn't really know the difference between feeling happy and feeling sad, and that might make things pretty boring. Sometimes we have a lousy day where things go wrong, or we have a fight with a friend or we might have to say goodbye to someone we will miss. These things can make us feel low for a short time. Some people say 'I'm so depressed!' but what they mean is that they are feeling a bit low right now and the feeling usually goes away after a few hours or a couple of days.

But what if the low feeling lasts for longer?

Some people feel low for longer (at least two weeks and sometimes much, much longer) and they tend to feel this way on most days. They may also start to experience other symptoms because of the depression.

This is a good clue that they might have what is known as **clinical depression** (or depressive illness). All this means is that their low mood has been around for long enough and is bad enough that it is stopping them from enjoying life, and basically messing things up for them.

How long have you been feeling low?

☑

Days ☐
Weeks ☐
Months ☐
Longer? ☐

Symptoms of depression:

Feeling low or sad a lot of the time ☐

Not enjoying things you used to enjoy ☐

Often feeling irritable or angry ☐

Trouble sleeping or sleeping too much ☐

Feeling worthless or no good ☐

Feeling very tired, having no energy ☐

Experiencing a big change in weight ☐

Feeling overly guilty ☐

Having no appetite or eating much more than usual ☐

Being unable to make decisions ☐

Being unable to concentrate or think straight ☐

Feeling restless or agitated ☐

Being much slower in your actions and when moving ☐
around

Feeling hopeless about the future ☐

Having thoughts about death ☐

Having thoughts about hurting yourself ☐

Having thoughts about suicide ☐

Do you experience any of these symptoms? ☐

Your total = ☐

Not everyone with depression has all of these but if they have five or more (including one or both of the first two), almost every day, for at least a couple of weeks then these are even more clues that they have clinical depression. If you have fewer than five symptoms it may mean that you have a milder form of depression.

Clinical depression summary

- One or both of the first two symptoms (feeling low and not enjoying things)
- At least five depression symptoms altogether.

For at least two weeks, almost every day and for more time than not.

How many of these points apply to you? If they all apply then it is pretty certain that what you are experiencing is clinical depression. The more symptoms you have, the longer they have been around and the more they affect your life, the more severe your depression is.

If only some of these points apply to you then this may mean that you have a milder form of depression or low mood. This may mean you only experience a few symptoms that haven't been around very long and they seem to come and go.

My mood summary

(Circle the answers that apply to you)

Do I have one or both of the first two symptoms?

Yes, I have both (low mood and loss of interest)

I have one of these _____

_____

No, I don't have either of these

Total number of my depression symptoms _____

_____

Is this total at least five?

Yes

No

How long have I felt like this?

_____

_____

_____

Has it been at least two weeks?

Yes

No

Do I feel like this and have these symptoms most of the time?

Most of the time

About half the time

Less than half the time

It comes and goes

How much does it mess things up for me in my life?

A lot!

A bit

Not much

Other possible signs of depression

- Feeling completely alone.
- Often tearful.
- Unable to cry.
- Feeling numb or empty.
- Feeling like you just can't cope.

- No motivation for anything.
- Feeling trapped.
- Losing confidence in yourself.
- Physical symptoms like aches and pains.
- Wanting to be alone all the time.
- Urges to self-harm.

Checking your own symptoms using a depression questionnaire

You can also check your depression symptoms using the **depression questionnaire** below. This questionnaire has been used by many young people and checked by doctors and therapists. It has been shown to be very useful in identifying young people with depression. It can also show if depression and low mood is getting better or worse.

Have a go at completing the questionnaire now if you like. You can add the items together to give you a total score.

For every item:

Not true = 0

Sometimes = 1

True = 2

The higher the score, the more likely it is that you have depression.

My first total score _____ Date _____

It is a good idea to then go back to the questionnaire at a later time and see whether your score is changing, especially as you use the strategies in this book.

My second total score _____ Date _____

My third total score _____ Date _____

My fourth total score _____ Date _____

My fifth total score _____ Date _____

Short Mood and Feelings Questionnaire (SMFQ)

This form is about how you might have been feeling or acting recently. For each question, please tick how much you have felt or acted this way **over the past two weeks.** If a sentence was true about you most of the time tick **true.** If it was only sometimes true, tick **sometimes.** If a sentence was not true about you, tick **not true.**

	Not true	Some-times	True
1. I felt miserable or unhappy			
2. I didn't enjoy anything at all			
3. I felt so tired I just sat around and did nothing			
4. I was very restless			
5. I felt I was no good any more			
6. I cried a lot			
7. I found it hard to think properly and concentrate			
8. I hated myself			
9. I was a bad person			
10. I felt lonely			
11. I thought nobody really loved me			
12. I thought I could never be as good as other kids			
13. I did everything wrong			
Short Mood and Feelings Questionnaire (SMFQ); Angold & Costello, 1987			

Total Score:

If your depression is severe and you are not already receiving professional help then please read this. If your symptoms are affecting you so much that you are finding it difficult to do most things, and if you are feeling hopeless and experiencing suicidal thoughts then it is very important that you let someone know immediately. This could be your parents, a teacher or your GP. You will need additional help from health professionals who have experience in helping people like you (Appendix 2 at the back of the book provides information on how to find a therapist). Please also have a look at **Chapter 3** now. You can use the strategies in this book to help you but this will need to be in addition to receiving professional help. Do not be ashamed to ask for help, everyone needs extra support from time to time.

How do I talk to my GP?

Some people feel worried, embarrassed or unsure about talking to their GP about their mood. Let us first reassure you that GPs are very used to talking to people about their mood and about depression. They talk to hundreds of people about this all the time. It is a very good idea to let your GP know how you are feeling because they can help you to find additional support if you need it.

- Before your appointment, make a list of symptoms that you have been experiencing (use the information on p. 7 or p. 13 to help you identify your symptoms).
- Also note down approximately how long you have been feeling this way.
- When you make the GP appointment it is a good idea to ask for a double appointment so that you get a little more time to talk things through fully.

- If possible, go to the appointment with someone else. This could be a parent, a relative or another adult you trust.
- Tell your GP that you have been feeling low or depressed and that you have noticed other symptoms (you can take this book along with your **mood summary** on p. 9 to help you explain your situation). Tell the GP how long you have been feeling this way.
- Tell your GP if you have been experiencing any thoughts about harming yourself or if have actually hurt yourself in any way (also see Chapter 3 in this book).
- Ask your GP if there are any talking therapies available in your area and, if appropriate, ask how you can access this support and how long you need to wait.
- Ask any questions about medication if this applies to you.
- Agree a plan with the GP about how your depression will be treated and when you should come back for a follow-up appointment.

A note about medication for depression

You may have heard that there are different medicines available to treat depression. These medicines are referred to as **anti-depressants.** For some people medication can be quite helpful, especially if they are experiencing very severe symptoms. Every person is different and some medicines work well for some people and less well for others. Some people experience side effects from medicines. These are effects from the medication that are not wanted, such as feeling a bit sick. It's important to remember that anti-depressants take several weeks to show any positive effects on mood and sometimes the unwanted side effects go away in a few days or weeks too.

While medication is a good idea for some people with depression, especially if they have tried other options, it is usually not the full answer to overcoming depression. Learning helpful coping strategies and making positive changes in your life are much more important and long lasting. For some people a combination of both medication and using strategies such as the ones in this book may be the most helpful approach at the time.

If you would like to know more about anti-depressants and whether they are right for you, talk to your GP about this.

Young people eighteen years old or younger usually need to see a specialist doctor at a Child and Adolescent Mental Health Services (CAMHS) to be prescribed medication for their depression. Your GP can discuss this option with you and your family.

Is there any good news about depression in teenagers?

The short answer is **yes**. For some people, the depression and symptoms go away on their own after some time and these people do not need additional help or treatment. For some of these people unfortunately the depression comes back later if they haven't had any treatment. Other people may need some additional help and there are several treatments that can work well. The ideas in this book are based on one of these treatments.

There are also other places and people who can offer additional help and this book provides some ideas about where to find this extra help (see Appendix 1 p. 311).

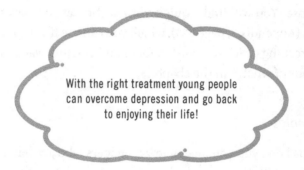

With the right treatment young people can overcome depression and go back to enjoying their life!

What will this book be like?

Self-help

This book uses a self-help approach. This basically means that we believe there are many things you can do to help yourself feel better. We want to tell you about them so you can try them out. The ideas are based on a treatment called Cognitive Behaviour Therapy (**CBT**). You will find out more about CBT later on, but basically it is a treatment based on the idea that our thoughts, feelings and behaviours are linked. When we can understand these links we can then do something about them to make positive changes. People have found CBT to be a useful treatment for low mood and depression. Because CBT is supported by a lot of research showing that it is effective it is recommended as a 'first-line' treatment for depression in young people.

Dip in and out

It can be hard to concentrate when you are feeling down, therefore the aim is for this book to be easy to flip through and use. You will find a **quick view** section at the back of the book (Appendix 3, page 329), which you can use if you don't feel like reading or it's too hard to focus and you just want to get a flavour of what is in the chapters.

Examples

In this book you will meet a few teenagers who are having difficulties with their mood. These teenagers will talk about their problems and the ways that they have coped. Hopefully you will be able to relate to some of their difficulties and perhaps try out for yourself some of the things that helped them.

Things to try

Throughout the book there will be some lists to look at and short worksheets to fill out. Don't worry, these will be pretty easy and won't take much time at all. We will also make suggestions about things you can try out in your everyday life.

Want more information?

In some sections you will find **Want to know more?** boxes. So, if you want to find out more about something then this is the place to look. Some people will look up the information in the boxes, some won't. It doesn't matter, but it's there if you want it.

Strategies

There are lots of strategies suggested in this book. Some of these will work for some people but won't work for others. You too may find that some are helpful to you and others less so. That's OK. Pick the ones that you like and that you find helpful. The strategies work best when you use them as often as possible. The more you use them, the better they will work. But don't feel pressured to use everything at once or to fill out all of the worksheets. It's up to you how long you want to spend on the strategies and what you want to try. Most of all, be patient and take one tiny step at a time. With patience, kindness and understanding towards yourself you can **overcome** depression!

Want to know more?

- If you want more information about depression in young people and effective treatments go to: www. nice.org.uk/guidance/QS48

- Another good website for more info on depression is: www.youngminds.org.uk. Or try this one (fact sheets about depression and other difficulties): www.rcpsych. ac.uk/healthadvice/parentsandyouthinfo.aspx

---

So that's it. If you think that it's worth having a look through the rest of the book then have a flip through now and see if something catches your eye. It works best to then go back to the beginning and follow the chapters in order, but some people prefer to dip into different sections that interest them in another order and this is OK too. Also, remember the **quick view** section at the back if you want to look at a summary of all the chapters at once.

When people are depressed they often have problems with their concentration, which can make reading more difficult. If this is the case for you then we suggest you read this book very gradually, perhaps starting by just dipping into sections that interest you and then moving on to other sections when you feel ready.

Meet Robert, Lin and Emily

We now want to introduce three young people who have experienced depression. They are based on real people but we have changed many of the details and names so that their identity is kept confidential. We will talk about these three young people throughout the book as they attempt to deal with their depression and other difficulties. You may be able to relate to one or more of these teenagers. There might be certain symptoms or situations that will sound familiar to you. Depression can be very different for every individual, although as you know there are some common symptoms that a lot of people experience.

We have highlighted in **bold** some of the things described by these three teenagers that could be **symptoms of depression**. See if any of these apply to you.

Robert

My name is Rob and I'm nearly eighteen years old now. I live with my mum and older sister. My older brother has his own place. My dad lives with another family. He drives lorries for a living. My mum is a dinner lady at school. All the bad stuff started about two years ago, around summer time. I wasn't doing brilliantly at school but I wasn't failing every subject or anything, it was pretty normal for me. I played for a local football team and for a while, football was my life! Things were fine. I didn't really have any worries or difficult things to think about. I was just hanging out with my mates, seeing my girlfriend and playing football.

Anyway, a whole bunch of stuff happened, not all at once, but kind of over a whole year. First, I didn't get picked for the new football team. I couldn't believe it, I thought the coach really liked me. **I was so angry** for a while after this happened. Then after a while I **lost all interest** in school, even more than usual! My marks got worse and I started to **get into trouble** all the time. There were some kids at school that used to **irritate me** and my mates and we would **get into fights** with them. Anyway, Mum started coming down on me hard. She was on my back all the time about school stuff. One of my teachers had a chat to her about **my behaviour**. She told her I was getting into fights and that I yelled at one of the teachers. Then my girlfriend started **irritating me** and we had a huge argument, and then she decided to go off with one of my mates, Neil. This made me even **more angry.** I think I was more **upset** with my mate than with her. So then it was hard to be around some of my other mates because I didn't want to see my girlfriend and Neil at all. So **I stayed home more and just wanted to be alone.** I also started missing school some days and just walked around instead. This only made me feel worse and even more annoyed.

My sister and my mum would constantly be on at me for one thing or another and we used to have loads of arguments. **I felt really alone**, as if no one cared. **I started to think that what was the point of me even being around** anymore. That's when things really hit rock bottom. I wasn't getting along with anyone and **I didn't want to do anything and nothing was fun anymore. I kept to myself** and just basically listened to my music on my headphones all the time. I was missing school and this got me into more trouble. I used to play on the Xbox all the time, sometimes for most of the night. Then **I would sleep all morning** and not get up for school. **I went off food** and just ate crisps, pizza and chips, and drank lots of fizzy drinks. A couple of times I bought some strong beers and just got drunk by myself in my room to block everything out. **I hated everything and everyone.**

Robert described quite a few symptoms of depression, as shown in bold above. One of his main symptoms was anger and irritability. Some people are surprised that depression can show up in this way. For some people it is not just about feeling sad.

Lin

I'm Lin. I'm sixteen. I live at home with my mum and dad and my younger brother, Sam. My older sister Kim is at university in London studying medicine. She's really clever and good at everything. She used to be really sad all the time but she is feeling better now. We haven't always lived where we live now. Actually, we've moved around quite a lot. I was born in Hong Kong and we moved to the UK when I was six years old. My dad works a lot and we had to move because of his work. I remember moving from Hong Kong, I remember I didn't really want to move and leave my house and my friends behind. It was scary but also a bit exciting. Since being in the UK we have moved a few times. It's hard because I always feel like the new kid and I'm always having to say goodbye to my friends. My mum seems to find it hard too because she's been sad a lot, like my sister used to be.

Just recently I moved to a new school and this has not been easy. I really miss my best friend, Amy. We text and phone each other all the time but it's not the same. I'm a good student and usually I get really good marks at school but lately **I haven't been able to focus** on my schoolwork. I don't really know anyone well at this school. I don't know where I fit in. Everyone has been talking about a party in the summer that one of the popular girls is having and I feel like I'm the only one who hasn't been invited. I was out with my mum the other day and I saw a group of the girls in town. They looked over at me and they were giggling and I think they were talking about me. They must think I'm a weirdo or something. I told Mum that we needed to go and I got out of there as fast as possible.

I feel quite lonely and like I don't belong anywhere. **I feel like I'm no good at anything** anymore, not even schoolwork. **I feel so tired** all the time and no matter how much I sleep I can't seem to get any energy to do anything. I used to like clothes and shopping and writing and drawing and I used to really love going to dance and drama classes. Now it just all seems to be so boring,

I can't get into anything and everything is such an effort. Mum and Dad have noticed that **I'm not really doing much** and they keep making comments about how I'm just not myself. They say I need to try harder with my schoolwork and make some new friends. They don't understand how hard it is. I can't seem to talk to them any more because I just end up **crying** and I can't say what I mean.

At school I keep to myself. At lunchtime I stay in the library or I try to help my teachers so I don't have to sit in the playground by myself. I don't eat my lunch at school because I don't want others to watch me when I'm eating. Every time I look over at the girls in some of my classes they give me strange looks and they're always giggling and laughing at me. When I get home **I can't stop thinking** about this. It just keeps going over and over in my mind, and I feel like I have butterflies in my stomach, and **I feel so tired and unhappy.** I just go to bed when I'm like this and **I try to sleep**, at least then you don't have to think or feel anything. The trouble is that when I wake up I feel even more tired and unwell. Sometimes **I wish I had never been born.**

Lin sounds really lonely, doesn't she? But if you met her you might just think she was a bit quiet and shy. Sometimes it's hard to tell if people are depressed as they keep their sad feelings to themselves.

Emily

I'm Emily, I'm fourteen years old. I have one half-brother, William, who is twelve. He can be so annoying sometimes! My mum works as a teacher at a school near to where we live. My stepdad owns an IT business and he sometimes works from home. My real dad died years ago, when I was a baby. I don't remember him but I have lots of photos of him. I used to have a dog, Charlie was his name, but he got ill and had to be put down a few weeks ago. I really, really miss him. He used to sit on my bed a lot and whenever I was having a bad day he would always cheer me up.

I have a lot of family who live near to us. My grand-mother is just down the road and I see her almost every day. My aunty and uncle don't live far away and I have lots of cousins that I see at weekends. We're always getting together and doing family stuff. I get along with most of my stepdad's family. Lately, seeing the family has been really hard work and I'm **not enjoying being with them**. I go to a school about half an hour away by bus. Now I catch the bus by myself to and from school. I had to sit a hard exam to get into this school and Mum and Dad were really happy for me to go there. I don't like school much lately.

Some people at school have been really mean to me. There is a group of girls who also get on the same bus who keep calling me names. They sit there and point at me and then make really rude remarks about my hair and my family. The other day one of the girls grabbed my folder and threw it under the backseats on the bus. They were laughing at me and then they threw my folder out of the window. By the time I got to school I was **really upset** and then I just started **crying** in class. The teacher took me to see the nurse and I cried and told her that I was just having a bad day. This is the fifth time I have cried at school in front of the others. My friends tell me to ignore these mean girls but the bullies have now started on my friends too. The other day I saw that one of my best friends was talking to one of the bullies and they looked like they were quite chatty. I'm worried that she will turn against me.

I sometimes hate going to school and I tell my parents every morning that I want to stay home. I'm getting so many **headaches and stomach aches** all the time and I feel really ill. Mum has taken me to the GP and they did lots of blood tests and other tests, and the doctor was pleased because it all came back as normal. But I'm not making up the fact that I feel ill, I really do. Some days all my muscles hurt and **I feel too tired to do anything**. I wish Charlie was still alive so he could cheer me up. Some days I feel like **I will never feel happy** about anything again.

You might be able to tell that Emily is depressed and unhappy if you met her. Emily has had a horrible time with bullies and this is something that a lot of young people find gets them down and makes them sad.

You can find out more about Robert, Lin and Emily in the chapters that follow.

Want to know more?

If you would like to hear about other young people's experiences of having depression have a look at the following website:

www.healthtalkonline.org/young-peoples-experiences/depression-and-low-mood/topics

---

TAKE-HOME MESSAGES

Many people experience depression and when you have depression you can have a whole range of symptoms that can make things difficult in everyday life. It's very important to tell others about how you feel and to get support from people like your parents, relatives, GP, teachers, and other services and support organizations.

There are effective treatments that can help people overcome depression and the ideas in this book are based on one of these treatments.

2

Goals

What are your hopes for the future?

Before moving on to the next section, take a moment to think about your hopes and goals for overcoming depression and for the future, both in the short term and the long term.

If this book was worth your time, what would you hope to get from it? How would this make a difference to you?

Robert's hopes and goals

Robert's hopes were not to feel so low and angry all the time. He wanted to 'get back to his old self'. This would mean he was seeing his friends every week, playing football, talking with his family more, going to school and not getting in fights. He would be going out on his bike and just having a laugh about things more often. Robert hoped to be able to read about two chapters of this book. He wanted to know a bit more about depression and see whether there was anything that could help. This would mean that maybe he could figure out who to talk to about how he was feeling. He hoped that once he talked to others about it, he could then get some more help.

In the longer term, Robert wanted to get through school without failing, stay out of trouble, get a decent job, one day have his own place, get his driving licence and own a nice car, and maybe have a girlfriend or even a wife.

What about Lin's hopes and goals?

Lin wanted to feel happier and to have some good friends. If Lin was feeling happier this would mean that she would be able to focus on her schoolwork again. It would also mean that she would be doing things she enjoyed like shopping and drawing, and maybe going back to the dance and drama classes she used to really love. Lin also wanted to stop sleeping all the time and to have some more energy.

In the much longer term Lin wanted to go to college or university to study performing arts or drama. She wanted to do plays and stage acting, maybe one day even to be in films. Lin's hopes were also to one day get married and maybe to have children.

Emily's hopes and goals

Emily wanted the bullies at school to leave her alone. She wanted to feel better and not to have so many stomach aches and headaches. Emily wanted to be back to how she was before, which would mean that she wouldn't be crying at school all the time, and would be enjoying her time with her friends and spending more time with her family.

Emily found it difficult to know what she really wanted in the longer-term future, except she knew that she wanted to have lots of animals and maybe work with animals in some way. She also wanted to live close to her family and friends.

What about your hopes and goals? Do you have any of the same as Robert, Lin and Emily? Or are your hopes and goals completely different?

At first it can be hard to even remember your hopes and goals because things may seem hopeless. Give it a go and keep trying, though. Having some goals, and being able to imagine them, can help you to make progress and move towards those goals, even if it feels completely impossible to begin with. You might want to get some help with this by talking to your family and friends. They may have some ideas for you that you agree with. We have also included a list of ideas for possible goals at the end of this section to help you.

My goals

So firstly, what would you like to be different? (This can be a depression symptom you would like to get rid of or it could be something else that you would like to be different in your life, or it could be something you have stopped doing because of the depression that you would like to start again.)

_____

_____

_____

_____

You might say things like 'to feel happier', 'to feel less lonely', 'to be less angry', 'to be me again', 'to not cry all the time', 'to feel less stressed', 'to have more fun', 'to be less tired', 'to get along with my parents more', 'to see my friends more'.

This is a very good start.

So let's say that this change happened. What would this be like?

_____

_____

_____

And what would you be doing that perhaps you are not doing at the moment?

_____

_____

_____

Who would be there?

_____

_____

_____

How would you be feeling?

_____

_____

_____

Would you be seeing anyone more often?

_____

_____

_____

What else would be happening in your everyday life?

_____

_____

_____

Who would notice this change?

_____

_____

_____

What would they notice that was different about you?

_____

_____

_____

Now let's think a bit more long term.

Two years from now. How old will you be in two years? Imagine for a moment that you have been able to travel forward in time to this point.

How would you like to see yourself in this future? What would you like to be doing? Where is this? Who would be there? What would be happening around you? How would you feel? What else would be going on?

_____

_____

_____

_____

_____

What about **five years from now**? Right, transport yourself there now. How old are you in five years' time?

What would you like to see? What does an older, more positive you look like? What are you wearing? What are you doing? Where is this? Who is there? What is happening around you? How do you feel? What else is going on?

_____

_____

_____

_____

OK, that may have been really hard. People sometimes find it difficult to think that far ahead. But it's really worth taking some time to think about it and to make some notes, even if it's just one or two notes to begin with such as 'I have a job I like', 'I have a boyfriend/girlfriend', 'I've passed all my subjects at school', 'I've got my driving licence', etc.

If you have been able to think about even one goal then WELL DONE, you are now on the right road to beating depression.

Ideas for goals

Short-term goals	Medium-term goals	Long-term goals
Do more exercise	Finish school	Get a car
Join a club	Get a part-time job	Move out of home
See friends every week	Get a girlfriend/ boyfriend	Learn to play guitar
Go to a sports event	Pass my exams	Get a job
Finish a task I've been putting off	Make a new friend	Own a new computer
Go to a party	Learn to drive	Go to college
Have a meal in a restaurant	Save up for a new phone	Get married

Do all my homework	Get a new bike	Live in another city
Make my friend a birthday cake	Learn how to ride a horse	Own a horse
Get my mum a birthday present	Go on a trip abroad	Run a 10k for charity
Finish my coursework	Play football for the school	Take a gap year
De-clutter my bedroom	Help with the school play	Become a ....
Groom the dog	Go on holiday with friends	Write a book
Cook dinner for my family	Lose weight	Learn a foreign language
Read a book or magazine	Decorate my bedroom	Learn to surf
Phone a friend or relative	Visit my granddad every week	Do charity work
Invite a friend over to my house	Organize a birthday party for Dad	Buy a house

TAKE-HOME MESSAGES

Taking a bit of time to think about your short-term, medium-term and long-term goals will help you to move towards these goals and make faster progress. Imagine if you were steering a boat on the sea but you hadn't decided where you wanted to go. It would be pretty hard to make the right decisions about where to turn and how fast or slow to go if you didn't know the destination. Give yourself some destinations and goals, even small ones to begin with, and this will help you to get there faster.

Part 2

Looking after yourself

3

Dealing with difficult thoughts and unhelpful or risky behaviours

Are you experiencing difficult thoughts or thinking about harming yourself? Or have you already harmed yourself in some way?

Sometimes when people feel low or depressed they might have thoughts about death, dying or not wanting to be alive any more. Some people have urges to hurt themselves in different ways and others actually do hurt themselves regularly by, for example, cutting or hitting themselves. This is known as self-harming. Many people want to stop self-harming. These types of thoughts and behaviours are understandable when people are experiencing difficult feelings and feeling very low, and it does happen for a lot of depressed people. If you have been having these types of thoughts or have been hurting yourself in any way then it is important for you to read the rest of this chapter, or at least the next few sections.

Robert had started to think, 'What's the point of it all anymore? No one would even miss me if I was gone.' He started to think about dying from time to time. As his mood worsened, these thoughts came up much more often and then he began to have thoughts about ways that he could hurt himself. Robert got drunk by himself a few times in order to escape from his feelings of depression and anger. He also thought about riding his bike really fast on a busy road, without caring what happened.

What to do if you have these thoughts

1. The most important thing to do first of all is tell someone about these thoughts and/or behaviours, preferably an adult.

This could be your parents, a teacher, a relative or your GP. Your parents or the GP are probably the best options to begin with. No one is going to judge you and it will be a very positive thing that you have shared this with someone. This is the first step to getting well.

If it's really difficult to tell anyone you know then first have a look at one of the websites below or call one of the numbers listed:

ChildLine **0800 1111** www.childline.org.uk/talk/chat/pages/onlinechat.aspx

(Free confidential twenty-four-hour helpline and online chat for young people up to nineteen years old.)

Samaritans **08457 909090**

(Free confidential twenty-four-hour helpline.)

Papyrus HOPELineUK **0800 068 41 41**

www.papyrus-uk.org/support/for-you

(Free confidential helpline and online support for anyone concerned about a young person at risk of harming themselves.)

Some people feel embarrassed about calling these places and they feel worried that they won't know what to say. Some people will call and simply say, 'I don't know what to say.' **This is fine.** The people who answer these calls are trained and experienced in talking to people about these types of problems and they are ready to help. Many, many people call these numbers and talk about very difficult emotions and thoughts, and a lot of these people say that they were really glad they could talk to someone who listened to them, without judging them.

2. The next most important thing to do is to put together an emergency toolkit for times when things feel very bad. Follow the guidelines below to construct your toolkit (on page 61 and page 62 at the end of this chapter you can summarize all of these points): it's best if you put this together with your parents or another adult you trust.

Who is the best person for you to talk to about your thoughts?

_____

_____

Who can you call or talk to next time you feel very bad? (This might be the person you have chosen above or it could be someone else or one of the organizations.)

Write the name of the person/organization here

_____

_____

If they are not available, who is the next person/organization you can call or talk to?

Number 2 _____

Who is the third person/organization you can contact?

Number 3 _____

Are there any other organizations that you can turn to? (See the box on page 47 and summary in Appendix 1 at the back of the book.)

List the organizations here:

_____

_____

_____

_____

_____

What is the telephone number for your GP?

Don't know it? Google the name of your GP surgery and note down the telephone number, as well as the out-of-hours number if this is different.

_____

_____

Where is your nearest hospital accident and emergency department? If you feel like you just can't keep yourself safe any more you can walk into the department and ask to see the 'on-call psychiatrist'. Many people don't realize that they can go to the A&E department for serious **emotional emergencies** as well as physical emergencies.

Nearest A&E department:

_____

_____

3. What are the things that seem to make your mood much worse and that lead you to have more negative thoughts? These are sometimes called **triggers**. Have a think about any situations that cause you to feel much worse (e.g. spending too much time alone, listening to very sad music, being with people who have a negative influence, having a disagreement with someone).

Note down any triggers that you have noticed:

_____

_____

_____

_____

_____

Be on the lookout for your triggers and use the ideas in this chapter to help you avoid these situations or cope with them in a more helpful way.

4. Now think of **two** things that have helped to distract you in the past (e.g. listening to uplifting music, going for a walk, eating something nice, reading a magazine, playing a game on your phone, speaking to or seeing a friend or relative, watching a funny show on TV, reading a book, having a long hot shower, drawing or writing, having a hot drink, doing something else that you used to enjoy, etc.).

Can you think of some things that made you feel better in the past?

Thing number 1 _____

_____

Thing number 2 _____

_____

Thing number 3 _____

_____

Thing number 4 _____

_____

Robert decided to have a look at one of the websites on the list. He found out all sorts of information about depression and how it can make someone feel. He also discovered that other people have the sort of thoughts he had been having. Robert read that there were things that could help and he started to feel a little more hopeful. After looking at the website and thinking about what he had read for a few days he decided to tell his mum about his thoughts. This wasn't easy because he was worried that she either wouldn't really listen or that she would become really upset. He waited until she had finished with the housework for the evening and he just came out with it. Initially she looked shocked and like she was going to cry, but then she asked him a few questions and they talked some more. He told her about the website and she said she wanted to look at it too.

He also showed her the chapter in this book. Robert's mum gave him a hug and told him that she was glad he had talked with her. She said that they would find a way to help him feel better and she asked Robert to talk to her more often about these things. Robert felt relieved to have spoken about his dark thoughts with someone, and he liked the fact that his mum took him seriously and wanted to look at the website. Robert then decided to make a list of people he could talk to or call if he felt very bad and the thoughts got worse. He listed his mum, his brother and his friend Jason.

Mum – talk to her face to face or call her mobile: xxxxxxxxxx

Jason – mobile xxxxxxxxxx landline xxxxxxxxxx

Chris – mobile xxxxxxxxxx

GP – xxxxxxxxxxx

Samaritans – xxxxxxxxxx

He also put down the number for the Samaritans and his GP. He put this all on a card and put the card in his wallet, where he knew he would be able to find it, and he saved these numbers on his mobile. He then thought about his triggers, and he remembered that his thoughts usually got worse when he spent too much time thinking about his ex-girlfriend and when he was alone for too long. He decided to be on the lookout for these triggers. He made a list of things that he knew had distracted and helped him in the past. These included:

- Watching something nice on TV.

- Seeing my brother.

- Listening to my favourite music (uplifting, not depressing).

- Doing something physical, like going for a jog or doing some weights.

He put this list in his wallet too.

Dealing with self-harm

Some people do not necessarily have regular thoughts about dying or wanting to die but they do experience thoughts about harming themselves in different ways. Or they may experience a combination of both of these types of thoughts. Self-harm, such as cutting, burning, hitting or scratching, is usually linked with very distressing and difficult feelings. Many people describe that they self-harm in order to deal with these distressing emotions. For some people it may be a way of feeling something when they usually feel numb. For others it is about relieving feelings of anger, frustration or other emotional pain. It may also be a way of escaping from feelings of depression or shame. Sometimes it is about having some sort of control when everything else feels out of control, while at other times it may be about punishing yourself or letting others know how bad things really are, or taking out your feelings towards others on your own body.

There are also sometimes particular groups of people who encourage each other to self-harm. Watching and hearing about others who self-harm can sometimes make people be more likely to do those things too, especially if they are feeling quite vulnerable. This is really unhelpful for someone who is feeling low. If you know others who cope by self-harming we urge you to not spend time with these people or to interact with them via social media, especially if you are feeling depressed.

Is this something that you are trying to cope with? If this applies to you then spend a few moments now thinking about the reasons why you self-harm.

_____

_____

_____

_____

_____

Do you want to stop self-harming? Many people say that they would like to find other ways of coping and stop their self-harming behaviour. There may be many personal reasons why someone wants to stop self-harming. One of the main downsides to self-harm is that it does end up permanently harming the person in some way. This might be in the form of scars on their skin or it could be other marks or injuries. At the very worst it can be dangerous and sometimes self-harming can lead to serious consequences for the person. This can happen, for example, when a person cuts their skin seriously without meaning to.

The person's family and friends may also want them to stop self-harming for various reasons.

Reasons why it would be better to stop:

_____

_____

_____

_____

_____

_____

Below is a list of strategies and ideas about how to cope with distress and strong emotions without immediately engaging in self-harming. Have a look at the list and mark any ideas that you like the sound of. Then make a decision to use these ideas a few times to see if it makes a difference. Make a note of the ideas and place this somewhere where you will see it next time you have the urge to self-harm. The hard bit is stopping for long enough when you feel very bad in order to remember to use these other strategies.

Some alternative coping strategies for dealing with urges to self-harm

Firstly, if you can, take the things that you normally use to harm yourself with and put them somewhere out of sight and out of reach. Make it harder for yourself to be able to get these out.

Delay

This method really works for some people. The idea is you delay the self-harming behaviour by ten minutes. Set an alarm on your phone if you want to and tell yourself that you won't do anything until the ten minutes is up. When the ten minutes is up, decide to delay for another ten minutes and set the alarm again. Some people find that after delaying for a while, the strong urge to self-harm becomes weaker and then they can distract themselves with something else.

Distract

Do something else that will take your mind away from the thoughts and the urges. The best distractors are physical. So go for a fast walk, go for a run, turn up some music very loud and dance and jump around, run around the house or up and down the stairs, throw a pillow against a wall, punch your mattress.

If you have an exercise bike or treadmill hop on and exercise vigorously for fifteen minutes.

Use other less energetic ways of distracting yourself if you prefer. Watch something funny on the computer/TV, write down your thoughts and feelings, express these using drawing or other forms of art, talk to someone, look at one of the websites suggested in this chapter, do some chores such as hoovering or stacking the dishwasher, cry or scream into a pillow.

Safer methods

Some people find they still need to do something that they can actually physically feel before the urge goes away completely. So some alternative ways to achieve the same feeling, without hurting yourself, could be to use an ice cube on your skin. When you hold the ice against your skin for more than a few seconds it begins to hurt and burn, and it can give you a similar sensation to other, more harmful methods. The huge advantage is that ice will not cut through your skin and leave scars. Pinching your skin or snapping an elastic band against your skin are also less harmful alternatives.

Better safe than sorry

Sometimes when people are depressed they behave in ways that are risky. For example, they may get very drunk, take drugs, ride their bike very fast in an unsafe way, have unprotected sex, hang around with people who they know are not good for them, accept lifts from people who are drunk or from people they don't know, or go to places where they may not be safe. People say that sometimes they get to the point where they just don't care what happens. While it is understandable that sometimes depression can make people feel this way, these types of behaviours can have terrible consequences. People often say later on that they wished they hadn't done these things.

If you feel the urge to do risky things, try to ask yourself whether you would still want to do this if you were feeling better. What advice would a happier, calmer you give yourself about this? If your friend confided in you that they were taking dangerous risks what would you say to them to help them stop?

Strong emotions and urges do pass

It is important to remember that no matter how bad things seem on a particular day or during part of the day or night, these strong and overwhelming emotions do pass. Think back to other times you have felt very bad. Did the feeling stay the same for a long time or did it start to get less strong after a few hours, the next day or after a few days? Emotions do change and the way we think about things can change too. Keeping this in mind may help you to not do anything risky when you feel very bad. Tell others how you feel and use the ideas in this chapter to get as much support as you need.

Now take the time to fill in the **emergency toolkit summary** on the next page. Fill in as much as you can now and you can add to it later on as you think of more ideas. It's best to fill this in when you are feeling relatively OK. It is useful if you fill it out with the person you have chosen to talk to about your thoughts, or you can complete it yourself and then show the person your ideas so that they will know how you would like to be helped. Keep a version of this toolkit somewhere to hand. This could be in your wallet or on your desk in your room, or perhaps you want to put a version of it into your phone. Wherever you decide to put it, see if you can remember to use it the next time you feel very bad.

Want to know more?

Have a look at this website for additional information and support for people who self-harm:

Harmless
www.harmless.org.uk

My emergency toolkit

1. Who can I talk to about my thoughts?

_____

2. List of people and/or organizations I can contact when I'm feeling very bad:

_____

_____

_____

_____

My GP's phone number _____

3. Things to look out for and avoid because they seem to make my mood and thoughts much worse (triggers):

_____

_____

_____

_____

_____

4. List of things that will help to distract me when I'm feeling very bad:

_____

_____

_____

_____

_____

_____

5. My helpful strategies for dealing with self-harming or risky behaviours:

_____

_____

_____

_____

_____

_____

Avoiding unhelpful short-term fixes

Drugs and alcohol

Some people are tempted to use drugs or alcohol when they are having problems and when feeling depressed. This might be because the substances help them to forget their worries and painful feelings or it might be to help them cope with a difficult situation. The problem with these types of substances is that they only sometimes work for a short while, and they usually make the problems and the depression worse. In other words, they sometimes work as a short-term fix but they are also a long-term problem maker.

There are several further problems with using these substances to cope. First of all, they can end up making you feel like you wouldn't be able to handle situations without them. Someone might think, 'I can only get through the day if I have this drug.' So the substances end up robbing you of your confidence and making you feel even worse about yourself, which in turn makes your mood even lower.

Secondly, these substances can make it difficult to function well in everyday situations. They can have a bad effect on how you get along with others, how you do at school, what choices you make and who you spend time with. People sometimes spend time with people who they know have a bad influence on them but it seems OK at the time when they are drinking or doing drugs together. The same applies to the choices people make. It seems like a good or fun idea when using the substances but later on they regret their decisions and the consequences (e.g.

getting in serious trouble at school or with the police, catching a sexually transmitted infection).

Thirdly, drugs and alcohol also work on a chemical level in your body, and have an effect on the chemical messages being sent between nerves in your brain and your body. This can upset the natural balance of chemicals and can have a powerful effect on your mood. Drugs and alcohol also have a specific damaging effect on young people. This is because your brain is still developing. It continues to develop until you are in your mid-twenties and when you use drugs or drink alcohol this interferes with your brain development.

This book is not here to lecture you on the dangers of using non-prescription drugs or drinking alcohol (or smoking). You know all that already. But it's important to know that these chemicals have a strong effect on your body and brain, and on your mood and feelings. If you are using drugs and alcohol to manage your feelings now this will actually be making you feel worse over the long term. Alcohol, as you probably know, is a depressant. The act of drinking alcohol will make you feel more sad and low. It can also make you put on weight, costs a lot of money and stops you doing other things. Alcohol increases irritability and anger. It is associated with aggression, violence, accidental deaths and visits to A&E.

The message is that drugs and alcohol will not help you with your depression in the long run, and they are likely to make things much worse.

If this is something that is relevant to you and you would like help with this, have a look at the information and support sites below. Also, it would be a very good idea to tell an adult you trust or your GP about your decision to stop taking these substances. There's no doubt that your decision will be supported and encouraged by these people.

In this book we will aim to help you develop new ways of coping with your low mood and sad feelings, so that you don't feel tempted to use alcohol and drugs when you feel low.

Want more support and info?

FRANK: **0300 123 6600** – confidential info and advice about drugs (including live chat and texting service).

www.talktofrank.com

Drinkline: **0300 123 1110** – confidential information, help and advice.

www.patient.co.uk/support/

Alcohol Concern: For anyone concerned about their own or someone else's drinking.

www.alcoholconcern.org.uk

Adfam: support and advice for families affected by drugs and alcohol

www.adfam.org.uk

TAKE-HOME MESSAGES

Some young people with depression have thoughts about wanting to harm themselves, or about not wanting to be alive. Others actually do harm themselves in various ways or do other risky things. If you are experiencing these types of thoughts or doing things to harm yourself in any way, it's very important that you tell someone straight away and get more help and support. Use the ideas in this chapter to put together an emergency toolkit.

4

Looking after yourself – the basics

In this book you will find a lot of different ways to tackle depression. This chapter deals with some very basic stuff:

- Sleeping
- Eating
- Exercise

In fact, these three things are so basic that we all tend to take them for granted. We want to show you why they're actually basic **and** important. So important in fact, that taking care of the basic things is a really good way of helping yourself feel better and less depressed.

We also think the basics are really important because **you** are important. This chapter is really about making sure that you take care of yourself. When you are feeling low and depressed it is particularly important that you are kind to yourself. This means taking time to look after your health. Sometimes, when we are depressed our habits and behaviours change and sometimes we don't even notice. A lot of the things we used to do that kept us healthy just stop happening.

Remember Robert? He used to do a lot of things that kept him healthy without even noticing that he was doing them.

Last year, Robert played a lot of football. As well as making him feel good, playing football kept him physically fit, was a way to spend time with his friends, gave him an appetite so he ate well, and tired him out so he slept well at night.

How is Robert now?

- He doesn't play football any more – so he gets less exercise.

- He eats a lot of junk food.

- He spends a lot of time on his own.

- He stays up late at night playing on his Xbox – he then can't wake up in the morning.

These different behaviours have not *made* Robert depressed but they do make him feel worse and worse. They keep him depressed and feeling low.

Has your behaviour changed now that you feel low? Can you think of things that you are doing now that you would not do (or would do a lot less) if you didn't feel low? Can you think of things you used to do that you don't do now (or when you feel low?)

It's easy for changes in behaviour to creep up on us. Often we don't notice at all and the change is gradual. Also, when we are depressed we don't think we are important so we don't look after ourselves properly. Often we try to spend more time alone and so we miss mealtimes. We probably don't care as much about our appearance. After all, if you feel horrible and dreadful, what's the point? Depression can mess up our every-day life. We tend to do a lot less than usual, it can be hard to get to sleep and to stay asleep, and even harder to get up in the morning, we can lose our appetite and just not feel like eating. This all makes us feel even worse, with less energy and less reason to get up in the morning. It's easy to see how this becomes a vicious cycle.

The cycle looks different for different people:

Robert's behaviour changes

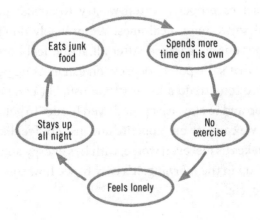

Emily had a lot of physical symptoms that made her worry about her health and meant that she stayed at home a lot.

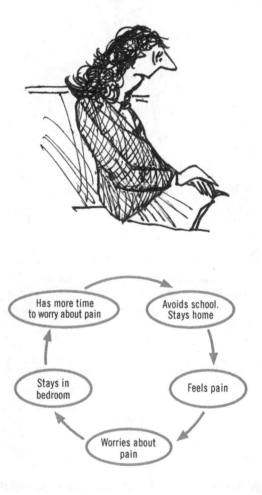

Lin tried to sleep to avoid her unhappy thoughts and feelings. She avoided being active and was tired all the time.

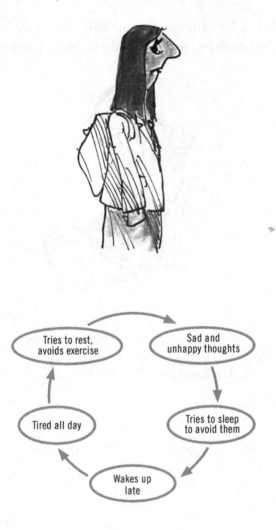

You might be able to work out what your own vicious cycle looks like – there's a spare vicious cycle below for you to complete:

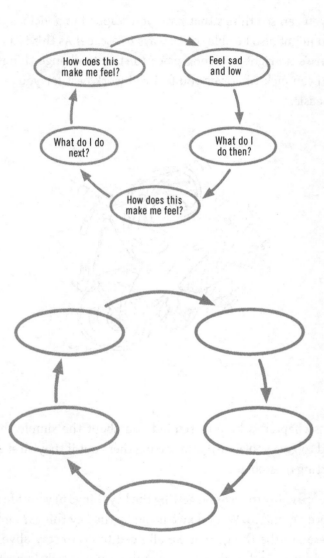

If you can see things that have you trapped in a vicious cycle you might also be able to see ways to escape! As this is a cycle there's no right or wrong place to start to change things, so you can pick whatever you feel will work best for you or will be easiest.

This chapter is here to remind you about the simple things and to give you a push into sorting them out if they've started getting messed up.

We are going to focus on getting the key things in your life a bit more organized. What do we mean by the key things? Simply, these are the things that we all need to do to stay alive and healthy. Even though they are simple they are really important.

Developing 'healthy habits'

Parents and carers are able to help babies and younger children develop good 'habits'. As a younger child your parents were in charge of when you went to bed, what you ate and drank, when you played, where you went and what you did. If you were averagely lucky you already have the basics of some 'healthy habits' that your parents gave you. Now, as a teenager and young adult more and more of these habits are your responsibility, your parents will give up some control and you will take on more control. If you were not averagely lucky you may not have yet developed some of these 'healthy habits'. Now as an adolescent and young adult you can start to take charge of your own life and starting with 'healthy habits' is a pretty good place.

Healthy habits are a way of keeping life on track. But everyone goes off track some of the time so they don't have to rule our lives. Don't worry if things go wrong sometimes – life can get in the way. At times of stress our habits can get messed up. But once you have set up your healthy habits it's much easier to get back to them when you need to. Also, the more we get into a habit, the easier it gets to keep it going and the easier it is to get back into the habit if we have to stop for any reason.

One other thing – if you find your healthy habits are getting in the way of the rest of your life it might be time to make a change. Healthy habits help us to get on with life. So if you find that your eating habits or your exercise habits start to take over your life – beware.

What we eat, how we sleep, how much exercise we get and what drugs we put into our bodies have a dramatic effect on our wellbeing. This is partly because they have a direct impact on our body as well as our mind. How we feel physically affects our mood and wellbeing – if you've ever had a significant illness you will know how this makes you feel mentally.

So don't think about this as stuff to do with being depressed. Think about it as just general good rules for life and it'll work. Everything in this chapter is good for anyone, at almost any time in life.

Did you know?

- People who sleep less at night also tend to gain weight more easily.

- Taking exercise improves your mood.

- People who are depressed are also more likely to become overweight.

- Sleep problems are a key symptom of depression.

- Sleep problems often come before low mood and depression.

Sleep, exercise, eating, drinking and taking drugs are all linked to depression and low mood. If you start by tackling problems in these areas it's very likely that your low mood and depression will also improve. So if you feel that you have too many different problems and don't know where to start don't be downhearted. If you start slowly, with just one area, this could help change things in all the other areas as well. In the next few sections we'll help you start with small steps. Don't be too hard on yourself – any small change is great. Make sure you reward any small steps and celebrate your decision to make a change.

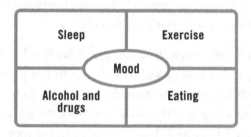

Tackling problems with sleep

It's very common to have trouble sleeping and it doesn't mean you are depressed if you find it hard to sleep. So it can be quite normal to feel this way especially around important events, even positive ones like family parties. The trouble with finding it hard to sleep is that trying even harder to sleep just doesn't work – does it? One or two nights of poor sleep is fine – most of us can cope with that and catch up at the weekend. But if you find that you haven't been able to sleep properly for weeks rather than a few days it's probably a good idea to try to improve things. In one study, young people who said they had sleep problems were four times more likely to develop depression, so lack of sleep can be an early warning sign.

How much sleep is enough?

Around eight to ten hours a night is probably about right for most teenagers, so nine hours is a good average to aim for. This is a bit more sleep than most adults need. Everyone is different so don't worry about what your friends say.

Do you know how much sleep you get? It is often hard for teenagers to get off to sleep and to wake up in the morning, and at weekends it's usual for your sleep patterns to be different. If you could sleep exactly when you want to you'd probably go to bed a bit later and sleep for longer in the morning – not surprisingly that's what most teenagers do at the weekend and during holidays.

During school and working weeks most teenagers don't get enough sleep. This is because their body often isn't ready to sleep until about 11 p.m. but their school or work routine means that they need to be up and about at 7 a.m. During the week therefore you probably sleep for less than eight hours a night and your body has to work very hard to fit in with an early start.

Facts about sleep

- It's perfectly normal to wake up several times in the night.

- Parents with a newborn baby lose about 500–600 hours of sleep – so have a bit of pity for your parents!

- Cats sleep for about 70 per cent of their lives.

- In the USA about 100,000 accidents are caused every year by drivers who fall asleep at the wheel.

What are the effects of poor sleep?

You might already know about these from your own experience. Short-term lack of sleep makes us feel tired, more easily annoyed and irritable, and makes it hard to concentrate, and also to learn and remember. Although we know how bad we feel if we don't get enough sleep, scientists still don't know very much about why we sleep. Luckily, though, we do know quite a lot about how to help people sleep better.

Sleep is part of a twenty-four-hour daily cycle – our 'circadian rhythm' or 'biological clock'. This internal 'clock' affects things we do every day, including when we feel hungry, when we are most alert and when we feel sleepy. If you have taken a plane to a different time zone you have probably felt the effects of disrupting your biological clock. You might have found it difficult to get to sleep, woken up in the middle of the night and felt wide awake, wanted to eat at times when there are no meals available, and even needed to go to the loo at different times of the day. All of these things are influenced by your internal clock. After you move to a different time zone it can take a couple of days to start feeling OK again – this is the amount of time it takes for your internal clock to 'reset' to the new time.

You can also alter your internal clock by sleeping and waking at different times, and this is what often happens when you are depressed. Robert found that he was staying up very late, until 4 a.m. or even 5 a.m. When he got off to sleep he then didn't wake up till after midday. Not surprisingly he didn't feel ready for bed at 10 p.m. when the rest of the family went to bed. After a couple of days Robert's internal clock got reset to a different rhythm from the rest of his family.

What is your sleep cycle like? Do you stay up late like Robert and find it hard to get up every morning? Has your rhythm started to look different from the rest of the family? Or perhaps you are more like Lin – if you remember, she tries to sleep as a way of coping with her sad feelings, but no matter how much she sleeps, she always feels tired. Lin has a different problem with her sleep – she goes to bed early, but wakes up a lot, lays awake thinking and worrying for hours, then when she gets up in the morning she still feels exhausted.

If you are not sure what your sleep cycle is like, why not keep a sleep diary? You can do this simply by using a paper and pencil chart or you can download an app for your phone. A sleep diary should include the time you went to sleep and woke up, the number of times you woke up in the night and for how long. We've included a sleep diary (see p. 82) if you want to do it on paper.

My sleep diary

Complete the diary every day. It's probably best to do it first thing in the morning

	Day 1	Day 2	Day 3	Day 4	Day 5	Day 6	Day 7
What time did you go to bed?							
How long did it take you to go to sleep?							
How many times did you wake up in the night?							
After falling asleep how long were you awake for during the night?							
At what time did you wake up (the last time)?							
What time did you get up and out of bed?							
How long in total did you spend in bed?							
How well did you sleep? (1 = very bad, 5 = very good)							

You can also find sleep diaries to download on the Internet – for example:

www.mpmhealth.com/workfiles/teen_diary.pdf

www.media.psychologytools.org/Worksheets/English/ Sleep_Diary.pdf

If you keep a sleep diary for a week that will probably be enough to give you a good idea of your sleeping pattern. But if the week wasn't typical, for example because you were on holiday, or you had people staying over and sharing your bedroom, it might be better to choose another week.

How to reset your internal clock

If you have trouble sleeping it's likely that your internal clock has started running on the wrong cycle. To get back into sleeping well it's important to reset your internal clock. This means that your internal clock is set so that you feel sleepy when it is time to go to bed and that you are able to get up refreshed in the morning. Resetting your internal clock can take a few weeks so it's important to be patient. The more disrupted your internal clock is now the longer it is likely to take to reset it.

If, like Robert, you are regularly going to sleep at 4 a.m. or 5 a.m. and waking at midday you are about five hours out of the rhythm you need. Assuming you live in the UK, you are keeping the same hours as people living in New York and Brazil. If, like Lin, you are going to bed earlier than usual, finding it hard to go to sleep, lying awake worrying and waking up several times during the night, your sleep/wake cycle is likely to be very confused.

You first need to decide what your sleep routine should look like. You should aim to get about nine hours of sleep each night, so on a school/college/work night you probably need to be asleep by about 10 p.m. Your schedule might be a little bit different, but for most of us early starts are a sad reality. It might be a good idea to talk this over with your family – they may be able to help you stick to your new regime, especially if you need help getting up in the morning.

OK, so say you decide you need to be asleep by about 10 p.m. and awake by about 7 a.m. This is your target.

The next step is to gradually alter your behaviour and habits so that you begin to move your schedule closer to the target. If you are five hours away from your target bedtime and waking-up time, you could start by moving your bedtime and waking-up time by two hours towards the target. After a few days you can start getting up an hour earlier and going to bed an hour earlier. Gradually move the time you get up and the time you go to bed.

It will be hard to get off to sleep earlier if you are not tired. This is why it is really important to make sure that you change your waking-up time first. If you wake up two hours earlier than usual you will feel grumpy and tired during the day. By bedtime it should become easier to go to sleep earlier, especially after a couple of days. The aim is to make you feel tired and ready to sleep at the target time.

Here are some ideas to try if you find it hard to get to sleep. Try these as well as starting to get up earlier in the morning.

1. Don't worry about not sleeping well. The more we worry about not sleeping, the harder it becomes to get to sleep. Accept that at the moment your sleep is disrupted but you have lots of ideas about how to improve it. Relax and know that it will improve in time.

2. Cut down on caffeine. This is a must. Caffeine is a stimulant – it can perk you up during the day if you feel tired but then it keeps you awake later and makes you feel tired the next day. If you drink caffeinated fizzy drinks, tea, coffee or chocolate, you are taking a drug that will keep you awake.

3. Don't drink any caffeine at all in the afternoon.

4. Your bed is for sleeping in. It's not a sofa, or desk, or table. Don't bring food or work to bed, or lounge around on your bed during the day.

5. Make sure you watch downloaded films, check your social networks, do your homework and use your laptop, tablet and mobile phone somewhere other than your bed!

6. Turn off all screens (laptops, tablets, mobiles) thirty minutes before you want to go to bed. Ideally put them in a different room. The light from these screens can keep people awake later on.

7. Make your bed comfortable and cosy.

8. Keep to a regular routine around bedtimes. Get up and go to bed at the same time, especially during the week.

9. Develop a routine as you get ready for bed. Try to make

this a quiet time so that your body can start to wind down. Have a warm drink such as chamomile tea or warm milk.

10. Remove distractions. Shut the curtains, turn off music or other media. Get some earplugs if you share a bedroom! Wear a mask to cover your eyes if your room is too bright.

11. Set an alarm. Get up when the alarm goes off even if you didn't get enough sleep last night.

12. If you are in bed tossing and turning, not able to get off to sleep, get up. Yes, that's right, get up and out of bed.

13. When the alarm goes off in the morning, get out of bed, draw back the curtains and get as much natural light as you can. Daylight stimulates melatonin, the sleep hormone.

14. During the day get into daylight when you can.

15. If you find it very difficult to get to sleep every night try going to bed an hour later. This might sound like we are contradicting ourselves but this is temporary. You need to be tired when you go to bed, so set an early alarm. Put the alarm (phone clock, whatever) over on the other side of the room. Get up when the alarm goes off and get on with your day.

16. During the day, do some exercise, walk, be active. This will help you feel tired and sleep better.

17. Make sure you eat regularly and that you eat at times that fit the *new* sleep/wake cycle.

When you are trying to get your sleep back on track you have to be a bit strict with yourself for a few weeks. Importantly, **at**

weekends do not stay up for longer than one hour after your weekday bedtime. In the morning, do not stay in bed for longer than thirty minutes after your weekday waking time. This will help you get into a good routine and reset your internal clock. Once you have had two weeks of good sleep you can start to be more flexible with your weekend sleeps. If you start having trouble sleeping again you now know how to get yourself back on track.

Robert found it very hard to change his sleep cycle. He had shifted it by five hours. Robert asked his mum to help him change but this was hard for them both because he got so irritable and snappy. They decided that they would gradually move his bedtime by an hour each day. Every day Robert set his alarm to go off an hour earlier. Some days he didn't manage to get out of bed when the alarm went off. After a while it started to get easier and his sleep cycle gradually improved.

Remember to let your family know that you are trying to improve your sleep pattern. It might be good to ask them for help. And also to warn them that you might be a bit more irritable and tired for a while.

Lin's sleep cycle was really confused. She spent a long time in bed. She went to bed as early as she could but then tossed and turned all night. She was in bed for eleven hours every day and even longer at the weekend.

In the morning when she did finally get to sleep it was hard to wake up and she felt even more tired the next day. Lin decided to start going to bed later at first. She planned activities to do until 11 p.m. at night for a week. Then she set her alarm for 6.30 a.m. and asked her mum to come and get her out of bed. As soon as she got up she dressed and took the dog out for a walk. The dog was very happy! Lin's mum helped her by making her breakfast while she was out.

Help! It's not working!

OK, it's time to get a bit tougher with the sleep regime. Try cutting out caffeine altogether for two weeks. You might be especially sensitive. That includes chocolate, we're afraid.

Don't smoke cigarettes or drink alcohol – nicotine and alcohol also disrupt your internal clock.

Don't take naps during the day – keep all your sleep at night-time and in bed!

Consider going to see your GP – just talking about your sleep problems to someone else might help you to see things a bit differently.

Exercise and physical activity

Feeling tired and worn out is often a part of being depressed. OK, you know that exercise is good for you but it might be the last thing you feel like doing. Even so we want to encourage you to start making exercise and being physically active part of your everyday life. Why? Well, there are two reasons for this. First, are the general health benefits:

Exercise – the pros

- Helps build and maintain healthy bones, muscles and joints.
- Helps control weight, build lean muscle and reduce fat.
- Improves your skin.
- Can help prevent or reduce blood pressure.
- Reduces stress.
- Improves your mood.
- Makes you think better and more clearly.
- Can help develop skills.
- Can be done alone or with other people.
- Boosts the immune system so you get fewer colds.

Second, hidden in that list perhaps, but hugely important for you now, is the fact that when you take exercise it improves your mood. After you exercise you get a positive mood boost. This is a temporary boost, but the other benefits of exercise will last longer – feeling stronger, fitter and leaner are all good for your mood, and your mental health as well as physical health. Exercise, on its own, without therapy or medication, has been found to improve symptoms of depression. Some GPs even prescribe exercise for depression – so the NHS agrees with us:

www.nhs.uk/Conditions/stress-anxiety-depression/Pages/exercise-for-depression.aspx.

Let's check how you feel about exercise.

a) I love exercise, it's one of the few things I can still enjoy, even now.

If you are already active that's great . . . keep it up. You'll already know that exercise makes you feel good. Having a regular exercise habit will keep you fit, help you sleep and improve your mood.

If you are exercising four times a week as well as being active in everyday ways – walking, cycling, taking stairs rather than lifts, then you are doing great. It's important to do enough to feel warmer, to increase your heartbeat and to be a bit out of breath. Give yourself a mental gold star. It's great to have managed to keep this going if you generally feel low in mood or depressed. You've obviously got some great skills already and can get yourself motivated and organized, so we will use some of those skills again as you work through the book. If you are doing exercise less than four times a week and you are enjoying it, why not step it up? If you are doing gentle exercise, e.g. walking the dog, why not increase the intensity? Maybe try something different for a change. This might be something to include when you try activity scheduling in Chapter 8.

b) I used to enjoy exercise but I've stopped and it feels too hard to get started again.

If you've stopped doing exercise, there might be lots of reasons for this. Robert used to play football but stopped when he didn't get picked for the team. This was one of the things that seem to have triggered his depression and he's not done anything active for ages. For Robert, exercise was not just a way of keeping fit but also a social event. He played with lots of friends, and he loved being in the team and working hard together.

If you've been low in mood and energy for a few weeks or months the idea of doing exercise again is probably horrifying. But you might be able to remember the upside of exercise. If we can help you get back into the habit of exercising or being more active, this will improve your mood and help you to overcome depression.

Our aim is to encourage you to get back into exercise – you might find some of the ideas we introduce later in the book useful to help you get exercising again. In particular, the sections on activity scheduling in Chapter 8, thought checking in Chapter 9 and problem solving in Chapter 11 will give you practical tips to try. We predict that soon after you start doing exercise again you will begin to notice the benefits, especially the positive effect on your mood.

c) I've not done any exercise for years – it's not something I enjoy and I'd feel stupid if I started.

Lots of young people stop doing regular exercise at secondary school and girls are more likely to stop being active than boys. There are lots of reasons why people don't want to do exercise. These include feeling embarrassed, especially having to change in front of other people, having to wear school sports kit, getting hot and sweaty, and feeling clumsy or not being 'sporty'.

If this sounds like you, you might remember enjoying running around and playing sport when you were younger – this is a good feeling to get back so let's think about ways of doing that now.

As you are someone who hasn't had the habit of exercise for a while we will try to give you easy steps to try out. We'll start with problem solving – and there's a whole chapter on this later in the book. If you'd like to get on with something now you can skip to Chapter 11 straight away. Problem solving will help you to figure out the main reasons why you stopped doing exercise. If they are still relevant we'll help you to use problem-solving skills to find other ways around them. If the main reasons aren't relevant any more it might be easy to get back into doing exercise. Or there could be different reasons now – again, problem solving will help you find ways around those too.

We predict that if you can get over the things that are in the way of exercise now, and you start trying it out, you will feel your mood improve after you exercise. Even if you hate the actual exercise, the hormones generated give you a mood boost. This mood boost doesn't last but it does make it easier to try again and to keep going. If you get into the habit of doing exercise this is likely to make you feel less depressed.

d) I hate exercise – I've always avoided it. I'm just not that kind of person.

If this sounds like you there might be two options. First, you really do hate all sport and all exercise, and you are never going to enjoy it. Fine, but let's just make sure that you move around enough to keep your body working and able to last you for the rest of your life. For you, physical exercise is just like car maintenance – important but not something to do more often than necessary. We suggest that you find ways to move more in your normal life. We predict that if you move more, even if you don't enjoy it at all, you'll start to feel better, your mood will improve, you'll sleep better and you will build stronger bones and muscle.

If this sounds like you then we will aim to help you schedule activity into your day so that it just becomes something 'normal'. You might find the activity scheduling section in Chapter 8 really useful. Also, we'll suggest you use the thought-checking section in Chapter 9 just to test out some of the beliefs you have about exercise.

Second, it's also possible that you just haven't enjoyed exercise – yet. School sports tend to focus on competitive sports and team games. You might be someone who enjoys individual sports, such as running or gymnastics, or non-competitive sports such as aerobics, or other physical activities such as dance or yoga. So it could be worth trying out things that you didn't have a chance to do at school. It might also be easier to try out new things outside school – for example, yoga at a local sports centre, or a club to encourage you to start running or playing badminton.

This might involve being creative and trying out things you've not considered before. Brainstorming can help with thinking up new ideas and is a technique we'll talk about more in Chapter 11.

So here's a summary – which type of exercise avoider are you? If you recognize yourself as a 'type', how can this book help you become more physically active?

Exercise type	Next steps
A – It's one of the few things I still enjoy	Give yourself a pat on the back – Keep it up!
B – I used to enjoy exercise but it's hard to get going	Introduce exercise into everyday life – activity scheduling (Chapter 8)
C – I've not done any exercise for years	Introduce exercise into everyday life – activity scheduling (Chapter 8)
	Identify the barriers and ways round them – problem solving (Chapter 11)
D – I hate exercise	Introduce exercise into everyday life – activity scheduling (Chapter 8)
	Challenge negative beliefs about exercise – thought challenging (Chapter 9)
	Get creative, identify new ways of being active, problem solving (Chapter 11)

Here are some advantages and disadvantages of taking exercise. Can you think of any more? If the cons are getting in the way of you being more active it might help to use the problem-solving tips in Chapter 11.

Pros	Cons
Teamwork	Get hot and sweaty
Healthy	Have to get changed
Improve/develop skills	Feel stupid
Makes me feel good	Can't afford it
Feel more confident	Can't do it
Make new friends	

Starting small

The idea of a physical workout can sound quite overwhelming when you are feeling low. This is especially true if you have a long-term illness or disability that gets in the way of exercise. But don't immediately write off the idea of being more active. Taking exercise can often help with the symptoms of physical illnesses.

What is really important is that you are as active as **you** are able to be. To be more active, you may need specialist advice to help you start to take small steps. You might need support from your family, from school or from a sports club to give you the help you need.

Activity is not just about moving your body around. It's also important to use your mind and to use this to discover new things and new possibilities.

You are what you eat!

Taking good care of yourself includes making sure that you eat well. As you are becoming more independent you naturally become more responsible for what you eat and have more choices to make. If you are lucky your parents have already given you some good eating habits and you enjoy food, and know what is good for you and what is not so good. If you are not so lucky and haven't yet developed good eating habits then now is a great time to start.

We all know that food is essential to keep our bodies going, to give us energy, to repair damage and build muscles, bones and blood. But what about our brains? Recently, science has started to focus much more on the effects of food on emotional wellbeing.

Research on food and mood is still new and although 'super-foods' sound exciting, we don't yet know if they have any real effect on your mood. But all food contains chemicals that have an effect on your body. We need food for energy, to build and mend our bodies, and to help our bodies work properly. You know that if your body is in good shape you will feel better and therefore we can be pretty confident that eating well is important.

Did you know?

- Your brain uses 20 per cent of your body's energy.

- Your brain cells use three times as much energy as other cells in your body.

- Eating breakfast improves your memory.

- It's important to drink enough liquid – but how much is enough?

- Your pee should be a pale straw colour. If it is any darker you need to drink more. Water is the best, cheapest and easiest drink.

- In the UK tap water is completely safe to drink.

What happens to our eating patterns when we feel sad and low?

Being depressed can really mess up your appetite.

Some people report that they eat more – especially more unhealthy junk food. Foods that are high in sugar, fats and starch give us a short-term 'hit' or reward. Because they make us feel better, even if it's only for a short time, they can become a bit of a comfort food. But the quick sugar rush with these foods can also lead to a 'crash' and an urge to eat even more of them.

Others find that they lose their appetite completely and that when they are feeling depressed they lose weight. You might also find that you avoid mealtimes with other people because you can't face them or you just don't feel able to be sociable.

Robert stopped eating his meals with the rest of the family and started eating alone in his room, especially late at night. Instead of eating the meals his mum cooked for the rest of the family Robert started eating a lot of pizza and other junk food. Not surprisingly, especially because he wasn't doing much exercise, Robert noticed that he put on a lot of weight. Lin didn't feel able to eat with other people at school and started missing lunch. She lost weight and not eating during the day made her feel really tired. Emily also avoided lunchtimes because she wanted to avoid the bullies. Because she didn't want to worry her parents she didn't say anything to them and when she felt ill, she also didn't feel like eating.

Do you recognize yourself in those descriptions? If you feel that your eating has become unhealthy while you've been depressed or low, or if you have never really developed good healthy eating habits, now is a great time to start to change.

How to build healthy eating habits

We know that when you feel low it can be hard to manage day-to-day activities and to look after yourself. Also, eating can stop being something you enjoy and start becoming a bore. While you feel low it's important to take care of yourself and eating is an important part of that. Imagine if you had been physically unwell for a couple of weeks. How would you expect to start feeling better? What would you do to help yourself recover as quickly as possible? If you didn't feel much like eating what do you think you would do to get yourself back to normal?

Probably you would try to tempt yourself to eat by having small amounts of healthy food. You would aim to focus on eating food you really like and you would probably try to eat small amounts of food quite often. You might also give yourself some treats – things you really enjoy eating and that might encourage you to eat a bit more.

Guidelines to healthy eating

This is not a diet book or a book about nutrition so we are not going to try and tell you what to eat. But, just to remind you, here are some basic guidelines.

The starting point here is to have a good balanced diet. What does this mean? Depending on your culture, where you live in the world and how much money you have, a mixed plate of food might look quite different, but should contain a mixture of carbohydrates (e.g. bread, rice, potatoes and pasta), vegetables and protein. Those are the building blocks of a healthy balanced diet. The plate below demonstrates the proportions of food groups we should eat to have a well balanced and healthy diet.

A Balanced and Healthy Diet

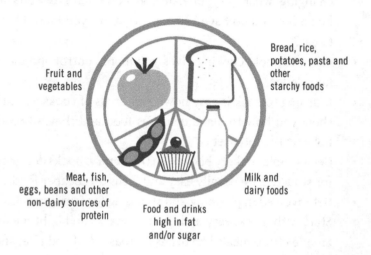

Fruit and
vegetables

Bread, rice,
potatoes, pasta and
other
starchy foods

Meat, fish,
eggs, beans and other
non-dairy sources of
protein

Milk and
dairy foods

Food and drinks
high in fat
and/or sugar

We understand that when you are feeling low you may not feel much like eating. You might not have much energy and other things may seem a lot more important.

So let's think about ways that you might be able to start eating more healthy food.

- If you are able to, eat with your friends or family. Mealtimes are important social events.
- If you can't face eating a large meal it's fine to eat smaller amounts. But eat more often to keep your energy levels up.
- Tempt yourself with smaller helpings.
- If you are tempted by junk food and snacks can you replace these with other options?

- Make it harder to eat junk. Talk to your parents about changing what they buy. If you don't have biscuits at home but you do have bananas, what are you more likely to eat?

- Learn to cook. Cooking gives you more control and more knowledge.

- Learning to cook is easy now – hundreds of cooks want to show you how to make delicious food and they all seem to be on the Internet.

- Get a simple cookery book from the library. Books designed for students are usually easy and focus on cheaper foods.

- Get involved in planning and shopping for family meals.

- Start with quick, easy and healthy snacks and light meals. Simple cheap meals like beans on toast, daal and rice, and boiled eggs and toast are fantastic and very healthy.

- When you feel a bit more confident try to cook something that you don't usually eat, experiment a bit.

- Cook for your friends as well as your family.

- Make your food look and taste good.

- If you are a bit fussy about your food remember that it can take up to five different attempts before you start to like a new food. So don't give up the first time, have a few more goes.

- Keep a food photo diary – this helps you keep a track of what you eat and will be a record of any changes you make.

Want to read more?

Here are some links we found which tell you more about food and mood:

http://studentsagainstdepression.org/tackle-depres
sion/healthier-daily-routine/understanding-food-and-
mood

www.mindfulcharity.ca/pdf/Teen_Resources_101.pdf

www.nhs.uk/Livewell/Goodfood/Pages/eatwell-plate.
aspx

TAKE-HOME MESSAGES

Making positive changes in basic things such as your diet, sleep routines and exercise can be very important and will help you to feel better and less depressed. It is also a really good place to start when you are ready to overcome depression.

Part 3

Getting started

5

Why me?

You may have picked up this book because you have depression or low mood, or because your friend or a family member seems to have depression. Either way, you may want to know more about why some people, but not others, develop depression. This chapter will explain why some people get depression and others don't. We will use the most up-to-date research and tell you what we know and what we don't know.

We can't cover absolutely everything in this book – this is a growing research area with a lot going on – but if you are interested in finding out more you can do more research and reading on your own. We have included a summary of places to find additional information at the end of this book.

So why *me*?

Depression is a puzzle in many ways. The word depression is used to describe a feeling or mood; something that almost all of us experience at some time in our lives. Feeling depressed from time to time is pretty normal. Depression as a mood or emotion will last for a few hours. It tends to be linked to a specific recent event. Depression as a mood or emotion will go away.

However, when we talk about depression as a disorder or mental health problem we really mean something that many people won't experience. It can be hard to understand why some people become depressed whereas others do not. Sometimes depression has a clear cause – something bad happens first and then the person gets depressed. But sometimes depression seems to creep up, out of nowhere, and strikes in an unpredictable way. This is because, like lots of other physical and mental health problems, depression has a number of different causes. Each of these increases the risk that someone will develop depression but there is no one cause that guarantees that depression will develop. We tend to think of the causes of depression as being biological, psychological and social.

The diagram opposite shows how these three things come together and influence your mood. In this chapter we will tell you a bit about each of these things and you can see if they fit with your own situation.

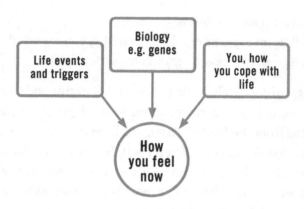

Life events and triggers – bad things happen, even to good people

Trigger events

Let's start with the most simple situation – a bad thing happens to you and this leads to a bout of depression which lasts weeks or days. This bad thing is a **trigger event** and can come in a number of different guises. Typical events that can trigger depression include the following:

- Moving house.
- Starting at a new school.
- Parents arguing/family conflict.
- Parental divorce or separation.
- Being bullied.
- Breaking up with your boyfriend/girlfriend.
- Feeling isolated and lonely.
- Feeling 'different', left out, shunned.
- Someone you love moving away.

- Having a serious illness.
- Failing an exam or not doing as well as you expected.
- Someone you love dying or being seriously ill.

Robert, Lin and Emily all had different life events and triggers. For Robert, it was a combination of a trigger event, being dropped from the football team, and then the feeling of being left out, lonely, and breaking up with his girlfriend. For Lin, it started when she went to a new school. She missed her best friend and found it hard to fit in with the other girls. Emily's dog died and she was bullied at school.

Can you think of any triggers in your life? These are things that happened shortly before you became depressed. They may feel like they caused your depression or that they were 'the final straw'.

Most people will have some of these things happen to them, often many of them and often more than once. Life is a mixture of happy and sad events, and everyone is likely to experience a mixture. There is some research to show that people who have more trigger events are more likely to report feelings of depression. But having a lot of very sad or tragic events does not necessarily lead to depression. Sadness is part of normal life, and is mixed up with happiness and other emotions. In this book we want to show you different ways of dealing with difficult feelings and trigger events.

Life events

A trigger event is something that happened shortly before we became depressed. For lots of people there are also 'life events' from further back in time. These can be things that affect everyone in the family, including deaths, separations, family arguments, having money worries and debt, or domestic violence. Or they can include things that affect a whole neighbourhood or even a whole country, such as being very poor, being a refugee, or witnessing violence or aggression.

Psychologists have noticed that things that happen to us early on in life seem to be particularly important. We think this is because the brain of a young child or baby is more flexible and malleable than that of an older child or adult. The brain of an infant or young child is growing and being shaped by the things that happen early in life. Therefore early experiences have a bigger impact on how the brain develops than things that happen later on.

Early experiences that are particularly linked with later depression tend to focus on our important early relationships with other people. As a baby or very young child our parents or carers have to look after all our needs. They have to feed us, keep us warm and safe, show us love and affection, and help us to become part of the family and the wider community. Sometimes our relationship with our carer or parent is disrupted. This can be for lots of different reasons – these include a parent becoming ill or even dying, or the baby or child becoming ill or separated from their parent.

Psychologists who have studied life events have found that (as you would expect) people who report that they had a lot of bad things happen are more likely to develop problems later in life. This includes depression but also physical health conditions like heart problems and stress.

One puzzling thing is that not everyone who experiences the same events will react in the same way. We don't completely understand why. Psychologists tend to think that what we learn about how to cope or manage when things are very difficult is important. If we manage to deal with the situation and eventually things work out quite well, we may learn how to solve problems, how to be strong and how to cope. This can prepare us for future bad events and gives us more confidence so we can cope. We are more likely to develop a sense of control over our life. So, for example, if bad events bring a family or neighbours together and they can help each other deal with the problem, they might become closer and be more likely to help each other in the future.

Thinking about your own life, can you remember any events that happened to you and your family when you were younger?

Did things turn out OK eventually?

Did you or your family learn how to cope?

Were you able to get help from other people?

TAKE-HOME MESSAGES

On average the more bad things that have happened to you over the course of your life, the more likely it is that you will develop depression. If things eventually improved either by you learning to cope and manage things, or by you getting help from other people, this might protect you against depression and low mood.

The biological causes of depression – DNA, genetics and the brain

You might have noticed that depression tends to run in families. When one family member is diagnosed with depression the chances are that they have a mother, father, sister or brother who is also depressed. Many different physical and mental health problems tend to run in families.

In your family is there an illness that lots of your relations have had? A very common illness that is partly inherited is heart disease. Doctors will always ask about your family history of heart disease so that they know if you are at a higher risk than average. Heart disease tends to develop when people are adults but lots of other health problems, such as asthma, can start at a much younger age. Emotional problems like anxiety and depression are also known to run in families.

This has led scientists to look for genes that might put people at risk of developing depression. So far they've not had a lot of luck. But this is because it's pretty complicated. Not many diseases, if any, are 100 per cent genetically inherited. If a disease was 100 per cent inherited it would mean that for any pair of identical twins both would always have the disease, or both would not have the disease. After all, identical twins are clones. They look identical, same eye colour, hair, skin colour and height. They have exactly the same DNA as each other. So if there is a gene for an illness, like depression or heart disease, and only the gene led to the illness, identical twins would have the same, identical illness. This does not happen with depression so it is definitely not 100 per cent inherited.

The other reason that depression and other illnesses run in families is because families share a lot more than biology. Think about your own family. Ask yourself these questions:

a)   Where do you live?

b)   How much money do you have?

c)   What do you eat?

d)   How much exercise do you get?

e)   How many friends do you have?

f)   How religious are you?

Chances are you and the other members of your family have similar lives. You are likely to have a more similar life to your close family (i.e. parents, brothers, sisters) than to your wider families (i.e. your cousins, aunts and uncles). But all of you in the same family are probably more similar than you are to other random people. Most families share a lot more than genes. Because our diet, wealth, physical activity and social support all influence our physical and mental health, we are bound to share similar risks of depression.

TAKE-HOME MESSAGES

If you are from a family where many of your close relatives have experienced depression, you have a higher than average risk of developing depression at some point in your life.

You may find other family members are a good source of advice and support, especially if they have experienced depression or helped someone else who has.

Many people who come from a family where depression is common do not develop depression. Many things, including their environment, life circumstances and/or their personality, can help to develop resilience.

There are many different ways of developing resilience and reducing your risk of depression. In this book we will show you how to become more resilient and protect yourself against depression in the future.

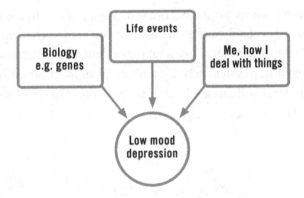

Me – how I deal with things

We now know that people who are depressed are more likely to have had bad life events, in the past and recently, and they are more likely to have family members who are also depressed. But we also know that there are differences between people so that some seem more **resilient** than others.

In this section we will talk about some of the ways people seem to be resilient. This is important because we can use some of this to help you become more resilient to depression. After this chapter the rest of the book will help you learn ways to overcome feelings of low mood. Also, we will help you develop habits which will protect you in the future and increase your resilience to depression and low mood.

Resilience

So what are the characteristics of people who are able to be resilient in the face of bad things and stay well? Researchers have looked closely at this and found that they have three specific things that seem to help protect them.

1. They have good **social support**. Social support basically means that they have family or friends who they can turn to for help. It seems to be more important to have a few really good friends or family, rather than a lot of friends who you don't know well. So, unfortunately, the 500 Facebook friends you might have don't necessarily give you social support – they could, but they probably won't.

    Having good social support in your life means that you can ask other people for help, and accept comfort and sympathy when times are tough. Social support is an important factor. We will come back to it later on.

2. They have balance in their life. People who are more resilient are involved in a range of different activities and relationships. They are the kind of people who don't necessarily put 'all their eggs in one basket'. In an ideal world we would all have balance across different parts of our life, including our work and study, our hobbies and activities, and time we spend with our family and friends. Balance also applies within parts of our life – for example, the balance between our friendships and our closer, intimate relationships. Someone with balance seems to enjoy a wide range of activities. If one part of life is going badly wrong, a person who has balance in their life is more able to access the good bits to help protect them. Activity and balance are things to develop in life and we will spend quite a bit of time on this later on in the book.

3. People who are more resilient are optimistic rather than pessimistic. That means that they tend to assume that life will get better rather than worse. They may not always be right, of course (!), always but being optimistic seems to be very useful in warding off depression. Optimism and pessimism are two ways of thinking about the world and we will be coming back to ways of thinking about the world a lot!

So, resilient people are less likely to get depressed when bad things happen to them and seem to have some specific characteristics which protect them. If we can develop these characteristics we can become more resilient to the effects of negative events.

The main aim of this book is to help you learn skills and habits that will protect you against depression and make you resilient. Our methods are all based on research that has been tested out both by scientists and by clinicians in the clinic.

Why me? – putting it together

So we've covered a lot of reasons why people get low and depressed. Hopefully you'll have recognised some of the things we've talked about and seen how they might have affected you. But not all of the reasons are necessarily relevant to you – as we've already said, everyone is different. If you are keen to figure out why you are depressed, or have been depressed, you might want to put together your own story. We've often found that this can be helpful. If you start to understand what led you to become depressed, or even more importantly what keeps you depressed, you can start to do something about it.

We can see how this works for Robert, Lin and Emily.

Robert

Life events	Parents separated
	Dad has new family
Triggers	Not picked for football team
	Arguments at home
	Broke up with girlfriend
	Lost mates
	Trouble at school
Biology	Drinking alcohol
How he deals with things	Spends time alone
	Avoids people
Things that protect or help	Has a close family
	Wants to get back to college
	Sporty

Lin

Life events	Family has moved a lot
Triggers	Started new school
	Misses her best friend
	Hasn't made new friends
	Not invited to party
Biology	Mum and sister have been depressed
How she deals with things	Keeps to self at school
	Sleeps a lot
Things that protect or help	Good student
	Creative

Emily

Life event	Dad died years ago
Triggers	Dog died
	Being bullied at school
Biology	Gets tummy aches
How she deals with things	Cries, worries
Things that protect or help	Has been able to talk to her mum
	Has some close friends

So now it's your turn – can you fill in the boxes below with your life events, triggers, biology and ways of dealing with things? Also, think about things in your life that might help keep you well or that you could use to help you feel less depressed. This might include people, or things about you as a person (e.g. being friendly, kind, thoughtful, likes animals, etc.), or about skills that you have (good at maths, able to cook).

Me

Life event	
Triggers	
Biology	
How I deal with things	
Things that protect or help	

So now you might have some ideas about why you have come to feel low and sad. Even more importantly you may have started to have some ideas about things you are doing that could be making things worse or stopping them getting better. We are going to come back to that in a later section of the book, so hang in there.

Want to know more?

If you would like to read more about depression, including causes, have a look at these websites:

Students Against Depression

http://studentsagainstdepression.org/understand-depression/why-me-why-now

Youth Space

www.youthspace.me/resources

6

The CBT idea

We mentioned CBT – Cognitive Behaviour Therapy – in the first chapter as a useful approach for helping people with depression and low mood. Here, we want to explain it in a bit more detail with examples and then encourage you to start thinking about how it might apply to your situation.

Cognitive means anything to do with our thoughts, including memories, wishes, plans and images (the things that go through our mind).

Behaviour refers to how we respond in situations (what we do).

Therapy just means it is a form of treatment.

Did you know that CBT is the most researched form of treatment for depression? It has been shown to be a helpful approach for many young people and adults with depression.

CBT helps us to understand how our feelings, thoughts and behaviours are linked. First of all, let's make sure we are clear what feelings, thoughts and behaviours are.

Examples of feelings

Excited, happy, angry, calm, frustrated, fed up, enthusiastic, worried, lonely, down, nervous, joyful, jealous, apprehensive, depressed, irritated, resentful, ashamed, relaxed, hopeless, etc.

In addition to emotional feelings, people often also experience different types of physical feelings.

Examples of physical feelings when feeling low

Very tired, slowed down, jittery, sleepy and drowsy, can't concentrate, wired, can't sleep, aches and pains, no appetite for food, etc.

Examples of thoughts

'I can't wait to go out tonight.'

'I'm no good at speaking in front of people.'

'I wonder why my friend hasn't sent me a text?'

'I might watch TV later.'

'My parents are so annoying.'

'I can't do anything right.'

'These jeans look really good on.'

'I'm hungry.'

'What shall I do tonight?

Examples of behaviours

Pick out clothes, get ready and charge mobile phone for tonight.

Skip class.

Eat lunch.

Keep checking phone to see if friend has sent text.

Go for a jog.

Slam doors when parents try to tell me what to do.

Shout.

Cry.

Keep away from others and stay in my room.

Complete homework.

The interesting part, as mentioned above, is that our thoughts, behaviours and feelings are closely linked, and if we can figure out these links, we can see if there is anything worth changing. And because they're all connected, a change in one often leads to a change in the other.

Let's see an example situation

Situation: Robert walks past one of his friends at college and says 'hi'. His friend walks right past and doesn't look at Robert or say anything back.

How does Robert feel after this?

Robert's feelings:

Worried

Sad

Confused

But is Robert feeling these things simply because of the situation?

The answer is **no**. It's how Robert is **thinking** about it that makes him feel the way he does. It's his **interpretation** of the situation.

Robert's thoughts

'He's ignoring me on purpose.'
'I must have done something to annoy him.'
'What if he tells the others not to hang out with me?'
'I don't have any good friends.'
'No one cares about me.'

Once we know what Robert's thoughts are, it starts to make a lot of sense why he would be feeling sad, worried and confused. **Thoughts and feelings are linked.**

What might Robert do (his behaviour)?

Avoids friend at lunchtime.

Goes straight home instead of going to football practice.

Stays by himself in his room at home.

Avoids town in case he runs into his friend.

Robert's behaviour

So again, once we know Robert's thoughts and feelings, his behaviour makes a lot of sense too. **Thoughts, feelings and behaviours are linked.**

But is that the only way Robert could think and behave?

What other thoughts or interpretations could there be in the same situation?

_____

_____

_____

Other thoughts

'He probably didn't hear me.'

'Maybe he's thinking about something else.'

'He's thinking about our football match and didn't even see me.'

'I'll catch up with him later.'

So if Robert was thinking this way instead, how would that make him feel?

Robert's feelings now

OK overall

Maybe a bit annoyed

A bit curious

So just changing how Robert was thinking about that situation led to a change in how he was feeling. This then had an impact on what Robert did (his behaviour).

Robert's behaviour now

Sees friend at lunchtime – finds out that friend's grandfather was ill and he was thinking about this all day and not really paying attention to anything else. (This explains why he didn't even see Robert earlier.)

Goes to football practice after school – quite a good game and Robert makes a good pass that leads to a goal for his team.

The low mood swamp

Sliding down versus breaking out

Changing the way Robert thought about the situation not only led to a change in his feelings but it also led to a change in what he did. This meant the difference between sliding down into the low mood swamp or breaking out.

Sliding down

- Think negative thoughts.
- Feel down.
- Avoid friend.
- Don't go to football.
- Feel left out and lonely.
- Feel worse and no energy.
- More negative thoughts.
- Avoid friends more.
- More lonely and bored.
- Feel more depressed.

Breaking out

- Think differently.
- Talk to friend.
- Feel a bit better.
- Go to football.
- Be part of team.
- More positive thoughts.

- Feel less down.
- More energy.
- Hang out with friends.
- Feel good.

Another way of showing these links is in something called a 'hot cross bun' diagram:

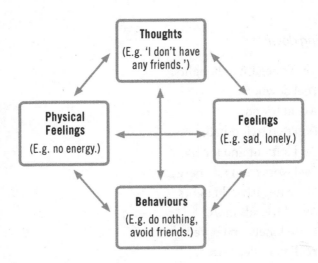

Because these four areas are linked, they can keep the problem going. So, for example, negative thoughts are linked with low mood, and feeling low can mean you are more likely to have more negative thoughts. Another example is that low mood can be linked with not doing much, but when you don't do much you are more likely to feel low. People can get stuck in these cycles and find themselves regularly sliding down into the low mood swamp. You might remember examples of these cycles from Chapter 4 (pp. 70–3).

132

How CBT can help

The way that CBT can help is by stopping some of these unhelpful cycles and creating more opportunities for breaking out. What we find is that changing one thing can then lead to changes in the other areas.

In the rest of the book we will be specifically focusing on helping you to change your:

Thinking

and

behaviour

in order to change your feelings

The physical feelings also tend to get better as your mood improves.

In the example on p. 129 Robert was able to change his behaviour (talk to his friend to see why he didn't say hello to him) and he changed his thinking ('my friend was just upset about his grandfather and it didn't mean he was ignoring me'), which meant he changed how he felt (less down). This helped him to break out of the low mood swamp (go to football and see friends), which helped him to feel even better.

Can you think of times when you have slid down into the low mood swamp or perhaps managed to break out?

We will talk more about this in Chapter 8. We will then go on to talk about how to change the way we think in Chapter 9.

Want to know more?

If you want more information about CBT and how it can help, have a look at the following websites:

Royal College of Psychiatrists

www.rcpsych.ac.uk/mentalhealthinformation/therapies/cognitivebehaviouraltherapy.aspx

BABCP

www.babcp.com/public/what-is-cbt.aspx

NHS Choices

www.nhs.uk/conditions/cognitive-behavioural-therapy/pages/Introduction.aspx

---

TAKE-HOME MESSAGES

Our thoughts, feelings and behaviours are very closely linked. CBT can help us to firstly identify these links in our own lives, and secondly to make changes in some things such as in our thinking and behaviour. Because they are closely linked, when we make helpful changes in one area, this often has a helpful effect on another area, such as how we feel.

7

I want to make more sense of my depression

Some of you might be thinking, 'Right, so I sort of understand how thoughts, feelings and behaviours might be linked and I kind of get that CBT can help change some of these'. 'But **how did it start and why is it hanging around?**'

For some people it is really helpful to understand how the problem started and what's keeping it going. This can be useful, especially when planning for the future. If we know what led to the low mood and what keeps it going, it helps us to know what to look out for and what changes to make later on.

You may have already started to make sense of the things leading up to your depression in Chapter 5. This chapter gives you a chance to think about these things in a bit more detail.

Let's think of depression and low mood like a burning fire. Stick with us on this for a moment! A fire will usually not start completely by itself and will not burn unless there are flammable materials available.

So the things that may create the right conditions for a fire might be a large wooded area, really hot and dry weather for a time, lots of dry grass, wood and twigs, a lightning storm, perhaps windy weather.

What are the things that might create the right conditions for depression?

These might be things such as problems in the family, bullying, sudden unexpected changes, losing something or someone important, high levels of stress or long-term anxiety, illness, someone in the family having depression, failing at something we see as important. It could also be our **genes**, so we are just more likely to get depression because of our genetic make-up. There are many other examples of things that might lead up to depression and you may have read about them in the earlier chapters.

So back to the fire. Once all the right things are in place, a fire won't usually start unless there is a spark to get it going. This might be a discarded cigarette or it could be a bottle through which the sun shines on to the dry grass and twigs, or it might be a lightning strike during a storm.

Is there usually a spark that starts off depression?

There can be. Some people can identify that **one** thing that really made them feel much worse. For others it's not as clear as that and it is more like lots of different things over a period of time. It's a bit like lots of small areas of smoke, giving off signals that something isn't right, but not actually all lighting up at once.

Once a fire is lit it cannot carry on burning without more of the right things in place. The fire mainly needs air and flammable materials to keep going. There are certain materials that really get it going, for example if we poured fuel over it, or if more hot, dry winds suddenly blew over it.

What keeps depression 'burning'?

Depression is very similar in that there are certain things that are sure to keep it going. Stress is a big one. Lots of stress is pretty much like throwing the fuel over the fire. So if someone is low and at the same time they are trying to deal with exams or if they are getting into lots of arguments with their friends or family, or if they are facing some very tough challenges or problems, all of this will be adding fuel to their depression 'fire'. The other main things that keep depression 'burning' are not being active, avoidance and unhelpful thinking. This is like constantly throwing dry twigs and grass on to the fire. The more unhelpful thoughts you throw on it the better it will burn. In the same way, the more you avoid things and withdraw from your usual activities, the more fuel you are giving to your depression.

How do we put out a fire?

Throw water on it or use a fire extinguisher. That's the fastest way of putting it out.

Is there a way to get rid of depression in this quick way?

That would be great if there was but unfortunately getting rid of depression with one move like this is pretty difficult. There are usually no quick fixes for depression. Some people say that doing some regular exercise can make them feel much better fairly quickly. So for some people exercise for depression could be a bit like throwing some water on the fire. This is usually not enough, though.

So how else would you stop a fire? Say you didn't have a fire extinguisher or much water to hand?

That's right, stop putting flammable materials on it. If you stop adding these to the fire, and maybe also start adding different things instead like sand or dirt to minimize the amount of air that is getting to it, eventually the fire will start to get smaller. After a while it will go out completely.

Things that can reduce the depression and 'put it out'

An important job then is to identify the 'flammable materials', that is the things that are keeping your depression going. Once you have some idea of what these are then you can experiment with changing these, or eliminating them altogether, to see if the depression starts reducing (a bit like the fire).

Below is a worksheet with examples to help you think about and understand your depression a little more. You can have a think about whether there were any things that made the conditions right for the depression to start and whether there was a particular spark that started it all. Then there is a space to think about what might be keeping the depression going.

Feel free to fill in as much of this as you want, or if it is too tricky or you don't feel like it right now then you can go back to it later.

Have a look at what Robert, Lin and Emily wrote about their own depression.

Robert

Were there things earlier in my life that set up the right conditions for depression?

Parents split.

Dad left.

Mum really sad for ages.

People not getting along in the family.

Was there a single spark that started the depression or was it a mixture of things that perhaps got it going?

Mixture of things:

Dad has new family.

Didn't get picked for football team.

Broke up with girlfriend.

Lost some of my mates.

Wasn't doing so well at school.

Got in trouble a lot.

What things are keeping the depression going now?

Staying away from people, especially mates.

Fighting with Mum.

Getting into trouble at school.

Not doing very much, avoiding things.

Thinking bad thoughts.

Staying up late.

Drinking alcohol and eating junk food.

What's stopping the depression from growing?

Still doing some things I like (e.g. music).

I still like my family.

I want to get better.

What needs to change to make the depression smaller or get rid of it completely?

Get some support.

Do more fun stuff.

Get back into sport.

See my mates more often.

Stay away from trouble.

Get along with my mum more.

Think differently.

Get some proper sleep.

Robert's hot cross bun example

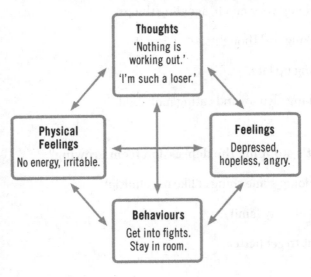

Lin

Were there things earlier in my life that set up the right conditions for depression?

Moved from Hong Kong and left all my friends.

Moved around from school to school.

Maybe my genes – other people in my family have been sad and Mum is sad now.

Maybe stress of moving all the time, having to make new friends and always trying to get good marks at school.

Was there a single spark that started the depression or was it a mixture of things that perhaps got it going?

Moving to this new school.

Missing best friend.

No good friends here.

Feeling lonely and left out.

What things are keeping the depression going now?

Not doing much at all.

Staying away from people at school.

Sleeping to avoid things.

Worrying a lot.

What's stopping the depression from growing?

Don't know – maybe me!

I have a good imagination, and I can sometimes imagine good times and come up with ideas.

What needs to change to make the depression smaller or get rid of it completely?

Try to get to know people and make some friends.

Do more things I like.

Worry less!

Stop avoiding everything.

Lin's hot cross bun example

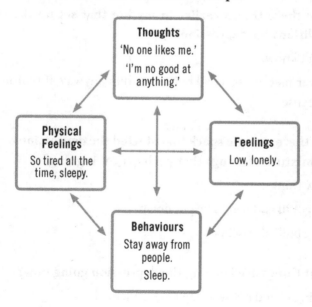

Emily

Were there things earlier in my life that set up the right conditions for depression?

I don't know.

I never met my real dad but I miss him anyway, if that makes any sense.

Was there a single spark that started the depression or was it a mixture of things that perhaps got it going?

A few things:

Dog got ill and had to be put down.

Being bullied at school.

What things are keeping the depression going now?

Feeling ill and not wanting to go to school.

Being bullied.

Crying at school.

What's stopping the depression from growing?

Sometimes I can talk to Mum or to my grandmother and this helps.

I still have some good friends.

What needs to change to make the depression smaller or get rid of it completely?

Stop being bullied.

Enjoy school more.

Focus on what's OK.

Emily's hot cross bun example

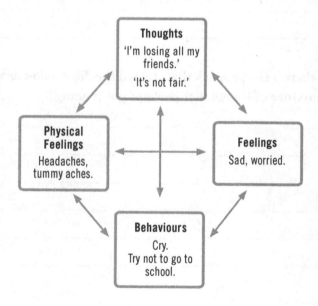

So if you feel like it, now have a go at filling this in for your situation. You can leave bits blank if you like and come back to it later. Also, as you work through this book you might find that there are bits on this that you want to change.

Were there things earlier in my life that set up the right conditions for depression?

_____

_____

_____

_____

_____

_____

Was there a single spark that started the depression or was it a mixture of things that perhaps got it going?

_____

_____

_____

_____

_____

_____

What things are keeping the depression going now?

_____

_____

_____

_____

_____

What's stopping the depression from growing?

_____

_____

_____

_____

_____

What needs to change to make the depression smaller or get rid of it completely?

_____

_____

_____

_____

_____

My hot cross bun example

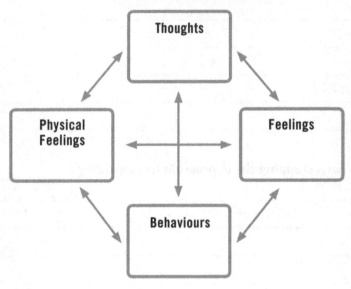

Don't worry if you don't know what to put into the thoughts box yet, Chapter 9 will help you with this. **Well done for having a think about this.**

TAKE-HOME MESSAGES

Depression can come about due to a number of reasons and it can be useful to think about the things that led to your depression. There are also many things that can keep depression going or reduce it. It's helpful to understand what these things are for you so that you can take control and make changes to feel better.

8

Feeling and doing

Tackling depression – doing more and feeling better

This section is all about becoming more active. We know that being depressed makes us less active. We also know that being less active can make us feel more depressed. That's a vicious cycle and once you are trapped in a vicious cycle it can be hard to escape. This chapter will try to help you escape from inactivity. It'll cover a few different things

- Why doing more will help you start to feel better.
- Starting an activity log.
- Identifying your personal values.
- Increasing valued activity.
- Using people to support you.

If you want to just get on with things straight away, turn to the section about keeping an activity log and you can get started on that. If you want to find about why doing more will make you start to feel better, read this part first and then start your activity log.

151

Your activities and your values

Things that matter to us reflect our *values.* Values are personal to you and are part of who you are and how you live your life. Some of your values might be shared by other people, like your parents; other things might only matter to you. That's fine.

To make it easier to think about your values in different parts of your life you can include three types of things:

- **You** (hobbies/fun, physical health, looking after myself)

- We've put you first because we want you to put yourself first. Try to increase activities that you will enjoy, or which will help you become fitter or look after yourself better. If you've already started sleeping better, eating better and doing more exercise, you've made a great start. These should all be in your activity log.

- **The things that matter** (education/work, things I need to do, the bigger picture)

- We all have things that we need to do. This includes working and studying. Here you can also include things you would like to do better, e.g. getting more organized, master a new skill such as learning to drive. Also don't forget about the 'bigger picture'. This includes doing voluntary work, politics, religious activities and working to improve the environment.

Feeling and doing

- **The people that matter** (family, friends, boyfriend/ girlfriend)

- Spending time with family and friends and offering emotional support and practical help are important activities that help others while helping us too. It is important to have support from other people when times are hard. It's also important to give other people support and help when they need it.

If you can find activities in each of those areas you will have a good balance, and this will help you to overcome low mood and depression, and be more resilient when you have problems.

Here is an example of Lin's life values. She didn't find it easy to think about these so don't worry if you find it quite hard.

153

My life values

What is important to you about each of these areas?

Me	Things that matter	People that matter
Hobbies/fun	**Education and work**	**Family**
I'd like to continue dancing and get a bit better	Work hard, do well at college and get a good job	Make my family proud of me, be a good sister
Keeping healthy	**Things I need to do**	**Friends**
I want to be able to be strong and fit so that I can carry on dancing	I want to be more creative and find time to write, Look after my family	Be good to other people, be kind and thoughtful
Looking after myself	**The bigger picture**	**Boyfriend/girlfriend**
Maybe I should make sure I do enough things for myself	Make a difference to other people – improve things	I'd like to have a boyfriend

Have a go at writing down what your values are in each of the different areas.

My life values

What is important to you about each of these areas?

Me	Things that matter	People that matter
Hobbies/fun	Education and work	Family
Keeping healthy	Things I need to do	Friends
Looking after myself	The bigger picture	Boyfriend/girlfriend

Why doing more will help you start to feel better

One of the things we know about depression is that it is hard to keep doing normal activities. Depression interferes with work and school life, with getting on with friends and family members, and with enjoying normal activities like going out, playing sport or taking part in other interests. Remember Robert? He used to be really active and very sociable. He loved playing football and spending time with his friends. As he started to feel low he stopped lots of his normal activities and began to spend more and more time alone at home. And what about Lin? She used to enjoy spending time with her mum and sister, going shopping, playing music and seeing her friends. Now that she is depressed she doesn't do any of these things any more. Do either Robert or Lin sound a little bit like you? What kinds of things have you stopped doing or do less of now? The list below includes common activities – which of those did you used to do? How many do you still do?

Activity list

Physical activity	Do now?	Used to do?
Swimming		
Playing sport (e.g. tennis, football)		
Dancing		
Other physical activity (e.g. riding, running, cycling)		
Skills/work/education	Do now?	Used to do?
Learning to drive		
Paid work (e.g. babysitting, paper round)		
School		
Homework		
Music lesson		
Creative things	Do now?	Used to do?
Drama		
Art (e.g. painting, drawing, sculpture)		
Playing music		
Cooking		
Writing (e.g. stories, diary, poetry)		

Being sociable/relationships	Do now?	Used to do?
Watching TV with family		
Having a family meal		
Shopping with friends		
Voluntary work		
Spending time with family and friends		
Having fun	**Do now?**	**Used to do?**
Going to the cinema		
Playing computer games		
Going to a party		
Having friends to stay overnight		
Planning a party or social event		

If life started getting better for you now, are there any things you'd like to do again, or even for the first time?

People who are not depressed often have a lot of different things they look forward to and enjoy. This means that if they stop doing one thing they always have other things to look forward to. However, people who are depressed tend to do much less. They spend more time alone, do fewer things that they enjoy, and have more time to think about their difficulties. Robert and Lin both stopped doing things that they enjoyed and started spending more time at home, mostly on their own. At home, alone, they have more time to think, more time to feel low and much less to distract them.

When you are depressed you can hardly recognize the person you used to be. And that in itself is depressing! We also know that doing less than you once did is a slippery slope. Once you start going down the slope it's hard to stop or slow down. Doing less makes you feel worse and worse, and when you feel worse you want to do even less.

Why do we do less and less when we feel depressed?

Being depressed is hard. Everything is an effort, things aren't so enjoyable and we feel rubbish. It's easier to just stay at home than it is to go out. Even getting ready to go out can feel like too much effort. Then if we miss something once it's a little bit harder to go back the next time. If we miss the next time, that makes it even harder to go back, and even easier to stay at home. Unless someone or something gives us a little push we gradually start spending more time at home and do less and less.

Sometimes there are specific reasons that we stop doing things. Robert used to enjoy playing football and spending time with his friends. Then he got dropped from the football team and one of his friends started going out with his girlfriend. Suddenly it was hard to go back and play football or to spend time with his friends. He felt embarrassed about the team – he wondered if he'd exaggerated his football skills. Maybe his friends and the coach had never thought he was good at football. Was he a fraud?

Robert was also upset about his girlfriend going out with his friend. He didn't want to be reminded that she now had a new boyfriend and he definitely didn't want to see them together. He decided it was less upsetting to avoid the football team and to avoid his friends. And in the short term maybe it was easier. But after a while he found he was stuck, he missed his friends and he missed going out but it was hard to change anything.

Avoidance and how it makes things worse

It's natural to avoid things that hurt us or are upsetting. We all do it and it can make a lot of sense. We avoid danger all of the time. As children we are taught to avoid danger and learn how to cross roads and keep ourselves safe. Avoiding some things keeps us alive. Sometimes we avoid things that we find upsetting or painful. This can be useful too.

But sometimes avoidance starts out OK but then starts adding to our problems. It can be like that in depression. Robert stopped seeing his friends and playing football because it was easier for him. To start with he did feel a bit better. He was relieved that he didn't have to face his friends and didn't have to worry about what they would think and what he would say to them. After a little while Robert missed all the good things about being with his friends and playing football. He didn't think he could talk to his friends about how he felt. He didn't know what to say to them about why he'd missed football practice.

Of course he could have joined another football team, or gone and made new friends at college, got a new girlfriend, or started doing something completely different like a part-time job. But these things can be hard to do, even when you feel happy and energetic. When you are depressed they can feel **impossible!**

So: Less energy + less motivation = less activity = Depression

Why doing less makes us feel worse

It's not obvious why doing less will make us feel more depressed. After all, in other situations, when we are physically ill, we are told to go to bed and rest. So sometimes doing less can be good for us. Why isn't that the case when we are depressed?

There are a few reasons.

1. When we are less active and do less we have fewer chances to enjoy ourselves. We get less fun. As psychologists, we would say that we get less **positive reinforcement**. Positive reinforcement is anything that makes it more likely that we will repeat an action. So, for example, if every time I go for a run I feel more fit and enjoy this then I am more likely to go for a run again.

2. When we are less active we are less likely to spend time with other people. Other people, especially our friends and family, are usually good at helping us to enjoy things. They might join in with fun activities, give us confidence to try something difficult or new, praise us or recognize when we are working hard at something, or make us laugh.

3. If we spend more time alone and do less, we have more time to worry and think about our problems and less to distract us from thinking about our problems. Psychologists have a word to describe the kind of thinking which people do a lot when they are depressed – they call this **rumination**. Rumination is a kind of stuck thinking – it tends to go around in circles and doesn't come up with solutions to problems.

Rumination tends to focus on things in the past and how they went wrong. It can include thinking like 'What if I hadn't . . .', or 'What if they had done . . .' Rumination is not problem solving – it is going round and round a problem without making any progress or solving anything.

Each of these three things combines to make us feel worse – this is the depression trap and it looks a bit like this:

The depression trap

Why start here? Why not change how you feel or think?

Remember the hot cross bun? Your emotions, behaviours and thoughts are all connected. If we change one thing, this has an effect on all of the other things. This chapter is about changing your behaviour. Why? Simple, really – it's because changing your behaviour is something you can do yourself.

But why not start with changing how you feel? Surely that's logical – it's your feelings that are troubling you most. You want to feel better so let's work on that.

If only it was that easy. People often think that's the place to start. It's why people sometimes say that people who are depressed should 'snap out of it', or 'cheer up', or even, 'pull yourself together'. Frankly if it was that easy you'd have done that by now and there would be no need for this book or for you to read it. So changing how you feel, just like that, is not an option.

Cheer up,
it might never happen!

OK, 'what about changing how I think?' Yes, your thoughts are important. Part of this book is about how to alter your thinking habits. But that's advanced work! Some people are able to change and control their thoughts but it's quite tricky and it can backfire. A good way of showing you how it can backfire is to ask you to do a short exercise. OK?

I want you to put this book down and then to think about anything you want for twenty seconds. The only thing you must not think about is a pink elephant. OK? Go.

1, 2, 3, 4, 5, 6, 7, 8, 9, 10, 11, 12, 13, 14, 15, 16, 17, 18, 19, 20.

Twenty seconds later . . . so how did that go? What did you think about?

- Did you manage not to think about a pink elephant? You did! Well, top of the class, that's amazing and very unusual.

- You thought about a pink elephant even though we specifically asked you not to! If you did, like almost everyone else, don't worry . . . that's completely normal. We are all very complicated and when we are asked not to think about something we seem not to be able to stop thinking about it.

Trying to deliberately stop thinking about something is very hard. This is why if you ask someone who is worrying about money or dogs, or spiders, or thunderstorms, to just stop, usually they can't. So, it's hard to control how you feel and it's hard to stop thinking your thoughts, so that leaves your behaviour – which we can work on.

How to start doing more (and then a little bit more) – starting an activity log

Before you start to increase your activities you need to know what you are doing now. The starting point is to keep an 'activity log' **each day for a week**.

Your activity log will help you:

- Find your activity starting point.
- See links between your activities and your mood.
- Spot times when you could start to be more active.
- Show you changes in your activity level as you progress.

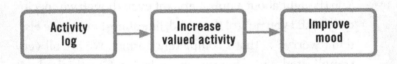

So what does an activity log look like? There's one on pp. 168–9 to give you an idea. It's also very easy to make your own. You can download these from the Internet, and you can use the diary or calendar on your phone if that's easier.

So let's get going. For the next seven days keep a log of what you do throughout the day. Don't worry about getting it right – this is for you. No one else ever needs to see it. You can always go back and have another go if it doesn't seem to work.

1. Record what you do. This means anything and everything, including things you might think are 'doing nothing'. In an activity log, there is no 'nothing'. So include things like sleeping, sitting on your own, waiting for a bus, or trying to sort out problems.

2. Then rate how it made you feel, from 1 to 10:

    a) How enjoyable it was – 1 is not at all and 10 is hugely enjoyable.

    b) Your feeling of achievement – 1 is not at all and 10 is massive achievement.

    c) If it made you feel closer to anyone or anything else – 1 is not at all and 10 is felt much, much closer.

    d) How important it was – 1 is not at all and 10 is very important.

My activity log – today's date _____

Date, time	Activity – what I did, with whom and where	Achievement	Closeness	Enjoyment	Important?
7 a.m.–8 a.m.					
8 a.m.–9 a.m.					
9 a.m.–10 a.m.					
10 a.m.–11 a.m.					
11 a.m.–12 noon					
12 noon–1 p.m.					
1 p.m.–2 p.m.					
2 p.m.–3 p.m.					
3 p.m.–4 p.m.					
4 p.m.–5 p.m.					
5 p.m.–6 p.m.					

Feeling and doing

6 p.m.–7 p.m.	7 p.m.–8 p.m.	8 p.m.–9 p.m.	9 p.m.–10 p.m.	10 p.m.–11 p.m.	11 p.m.–12 midnight	12 midnight–1 a.m.	1 a.m.–2 a.m.	2 a.m.–3 a.m.	3 a.m.–4 a.m.	4 a.m.–5 a.m.	5 a.m.–6 a.m.	7 a.m.–8 a.m.

Filling out your activity log

If you feel that filling out your activity log for a whole day is too much for you, try filling it out during the day, little bits at a time. You can do this the traditional way using paper and a pen – very handy! Or you might find it easier to log your activity using the diary or calendar on your phone. You can set an alarm on your phone to remind you when to complete the diary. Send yourself a text message to remind yourself what you are doing during the day. You can include the ratings as well.

It's tempting to think 'What's the point, nothing is going to help' – but just let that thought go for the moment.

Think of this as a bit of an experiment. If it doesn't help you've lost nothing. But it might help and you won't know until you try.

Why not ask someone to help you? A parent, a friend, or a brother or sister might be good at reminding you to fill out your activity log. They might also encourage you to do it when you feel like giving up – and that's really useful.

A completed activity log

So what does a completed activity log look like? Below you'll see a day from Lin's activity log. Don't worry if yours doesn't look like this – everyone is different and everyone's activity log will be different. Lin found it hard to rate everything – so rather than deciding how important her activities were from one to ten she decided to just say yes (Y) they were important and leave it blank if they were not important.

Lin's activity log

Date, time Monday 8th	Activity – what I did, with whom, and where	Achievement	Closeness	Enjoyment	Important?
7 a.m.–8 a.m.	Overslept – woke up late, felt awful.	0	0	0	
8 a.m.–9 a.m.	Got dressed, ran for bus, missed breakfast.	0	0	0	
9 a.m.–10 a.m.	First lesson – maths x 2, forgot homework.	0	0	0	Y
10 a.m.–11 a.m.	Break. Sat in library on my own. English lesson.	2	0	1	Y
11 a.m.–12 noon	English lesson, History lesson. Sat next to Emma.	4	3	3	Y
12 noon–1 p.m.	Lunch – ate with Emma. Talked about her gran.	0	6	4	Y

Feeling and doing

1 p.m.–2 p.m.	Science practical. Worked with Claire and Sam.	5	3	5	Y
2 p.m.–3 p.m.	Science practical. Got homework.	5	3	3	Y
3 p.m.–4 p.m.	Home on bus. Sat on my own.	0	0	0	
4 p.m.–5 p.m.	In my room. Felt sad, cried. Didn't do homework.	0	0	0	
5 p.m.–6 p.m.	Went to dance class.	2	4	5	Y
6 p.m.–7 p.m.	Teatime with family. Brother got school prize.	0	5	4	
7 p.m.–8 p.m.	In my room, supposed to be doing homework, cried.	0	0	0	Y

8 p.m.–9 p.m.	Watched TV with brother. Dad came home.	0	7	7	
9 p.m.–10 p.m.	Packed school bag, set alarm, had a bath, got ready for next day.	4	0	3	Y
10 p.m.–11 p.m.	Went to bed, said goodnight to family.	2	2	2	Y
11 p.m.–12 midnight	Couldn't get to sleep.	0	0	0	
12 midnight–1 a.m.	Tried to sleep, got up, had a drink, went back to bed.	0	0	0	
1 a.m.–2 a.m.	At some point went to sleep, took ages.	0	0	0	
2 a.m.–3 a.m.	Asleep.				

Let's have a look at Lin's activities. This was a school day so she was quite busy and a lot of her activities were important. Lin didn't enjoy much of the day but the most enjoyable part of it was in the evening when she was watching the TV with her brother. She spent a few hours in her room on her own, sometimes doing homework (or not doing homework).

Her day is probably not unusual. Lots of time can be taken up doing things we have to do – going to school, homework, exams, part-time jobs, hobbies and sports. All of these things are important but they can make it hard to find time to do things that are enjoyable or things that make us feel closer to other people. They can even squeeze out activities that we do just for fun. Ideally we'd have a balance between doing important (and unavoidable) things, doing things we enjoy, and doing things that help us feel closer to our family and friends. Remember that having a balance of activities is a way of being 'resilient' and being able to cope well with difficult life events and triggers.

We recommend keeping your activity log every day for a week at least. This is your starting point. Things can change from day to day over a week and don't forget weekends are usually very different from weekdays. If you do your activity log in the holidays it will look very different from during term time.

Making sense of your activity log

After a week what does your activity log tell you and what have you noticed as you filled it in?

Here are some things to look for:

- How many different things did you enjoy?
- How many of your activities were important?
- Do your activities give you a feeling of having achieved something?
- Do any of your activities make you feel closer to other people?
- Is your mood the same all the time, all through the day from morning to evening or did it go up and down?
- Was your mood better or worse than you expected (or about the same)?
- Was your mood the same every day?
- Did your mood change at particular times?
- What were you doing when your mood was most positive?

Starting to be more active

We hope you can see that becoming more active is important and that it will help you to overcome your low mood. In the last section you started an activity log and spent some time thinking about what mattered to you – your values.

Now it's time to do more of the things that matter to you in your life. There are a few reasons why it's important to focus your activities on things that matter to you.

1. Your values are an important part of who you are and who you become.

2. You are more likely to do things that matter to you; there's a point to it.

3. Doing things that matter to you will give you a sense of achievement.

Starting to do more and feeling better

We know that changing your behaviour and becoming more active is hard. But we also know that if you change your behaviour and become more active this will help you to feel better and less depressed. So it's important. This is where we really start to change.

Where shall I start?

This is a good question. In your activity log you might see lots of times when you could increase your activities. But how do you decide what to do and when? Have a look at your activity log and your values. How well do they match?

Values tend to be quite general and abstract. Here are some of Lin's values:

'I want to make my parents proud.'

'I want to do well at college and get a good job.'

'I want to be a good sister.'

'I want to stay fit and strong so that I can carry on dancing.'

'I want to be more creative and have time to write.'

How well do Lin's values match her activity log? Can you see any areas where she could add activities or change her activities to match her values a bit better? We can rate the match between Lin's activities and her values out of five.

0	1	2	3	4	5
No match					Perfect match

Lin's activities and values

'*I want to make my parents proud*' – Lin works hard at school even when she feels low. She puts time aside for her homework, even when she's not able to do much. Lin's parents might also be proud of other things she could do, for example, helping out at home, being thoughtful and kind, having a part-time job or doing well at drama. But to start with this is a pretty good match, say four out of five.

'*It's important to do well at college and get a good job*' – Lin is working hard at school and most of her day is spent at school or trying to do homework. She isn't able to work at her best at the moment because of her low mood but her activities do reflect this core value. Again, this is a good match for Lin, four out of five.

'*It's important to keep myself healthy*' – Lin went to her dance class and this is a good way of keeping herself healthy. It would be important to see if Lin is doing any other physical activity during the week. If she isn't then she could consider adding an extra hour of exercise one or two days a week. Also, Lin could think about other things she could be doing to keep herself healthy. Her activity log showed that she woke up late for school and found it difficult to get off to sleep so it is likely that she could change her daily activities to get into a better sleep routine. Because there are a few extra things Lin could do to keep herself healthy let's give this three out of five.

'*I want to be a good sister*' – Lin spent two hours with her younger brother, at dinnertime and watching the TV. Watching TV with her brother was the time she enjoyed most in the day. Lin could look for other times in the week, especially weekends when she and her brother could spend more time together. She also has an older sister who is away at university, so Lin could add time during the week to text or email her and to catch up on her news. This would probably be a three out of five match. This is a good area to consider adding activities because Lin enjoyed spending time with her brother so it might increase her enjoyment straight away.

'I want to be more creative and have time to write' – in Lin's activity diary there is no time at all spent being creative or writing. So this is something Lin could add into her activity log once or twice a week. Because there is no activity at all that gets a zero out of five. This is a good place to think about increasing activities because it will help Lin spend time on something very important to her.

What three simple activities could Lin add that would help her match her values?

Lin now has at least three new activities she could add that would be a good match for her values. There's no right or wrong place to start, so it's a good idea to start with things that are easier and things that are more likely to be enjoyable. She can then gradually add activities over a few weeks. It might be easier to add activities at the weekend, when there is usually more free time, than during the week. Or she could add some activities, like texting her sister, on the bus journey to school.

Lin's life value	Match	Possible new activity
Make my parents proud.	4	No
Do well at college and get a good job.	4	No
Keep healthy.	3	Yes – exercise more?
Be a good sister.	3	Yes – spend more time with brother?
Be more creative.	0	Yes – add one hour a week to write or draw.

Your activities and values

OK, so looking back at your own activity log are there times when you could start to increase your activity?

Are there any activities you are doing that are optional, which don't match your values and that you don't enjoy? If so, can you stop doing these or spend less time on them?

Looking at your activity log can you find something you did which matches each of your values? What rating (zero to five) would you give each value? Where are the gaps?

My life values

This is what I did (from the activity log) to match my values

Me	Things that matter	People that matter
Hobbies/fun	Education and work	Family
Keeping healthy	Things I need to do	Friends
Looking after myself	The bigger picture	Boyfriend/girlfriend

Do you have activities in every area? If you do that's amazing: well done! Chances are though that you don't. Do you have areas where your rating is less than three or four out of five? These might be places where it would be useful to increase your activity.

Can you identify three or four areas where you are not very active? Can you think of any extra activities that you could start to do?

Life value area	Rating 0, 1, 2 or 3	Possible new activity
1		
2		
3		
4		

Troubleshooting – getting started

You have a lot of choices to make about how to increase your activity. You probably have some ideas about where to start already.

If you are finding it difficult to decide where to start here are some ideas:

- Are there things in your activity log that you enjoyed more than others? Can you do more of those?
- Have you stopped doing something that you did enjoy? Why not start again?
- Are there activities that would help match more than one value? For example, can you combine doing something for yourself, like keeping healthy, with spending time with people who matter to you?
- What about things that are just for you? Things you enjoy – including creative activities like playing music, art or drawing.
- Check that you plan your activities to include relaxation, time for meals and enough time before bed to wind down.
- Try to include some physical activity every day. If you are able to spend time outside that's great.
- Make a plan. Think about the next seven days. If you can add one extra activity each day that is fantastic. Plan extra activities and write down the plan.
- Start small. It's better to do an extra activity for ten minutes and get it done than to aim to do fifty minutes and give up halfway through.

- Get help. Family and friends can really help us get going and keep going. So let other people know what you are trying to do and ask them to help you. They can help in lots of ways – giving you new ideas, encouragement, praise, general support, practical help, suggestions and by joining in with you.

Keeping going

Getting started is a huge achievement. You really need to reward yourself and to appreciate what you have started. Your activity log will show you what you have achieved and is an important way to track your progress. You will see what activities are going well and what effect different activities have on your mood.

At the end of each week, make time to look over your activity log and at how the week went. Here are some other things that might help:

- Involve others. Activities that involve other people can be harder to avoid so, if you can, plan activities with others. A bit of gentle peer pressure (encouragement!) to do something together can help get you over small hurdles that might otherwise trip you up and stop you. Also, you might be able to find activities that help you get closer to other people and match some of your other values (e.g. keeping healthy).
- Congratulate yourself when you manage an extra activity. This is really important and shows you have made real

progress. Build in little treats or rewards for yourself. You deserve it.

- Record what you did. Use the activity log each day.
- Increase activities gradually. Break things down into smaller steps and take a step at a time. You will climb up, step by step. Just like if you were climbing a ladder you can stop for a bit, or even go back a step, just keep your eyes on the top step. So, for example, if you don't do much exercise now but want to start doing more, don't start with a 5 km run. Start with something you have a really good chance of finishing. Beginner runners generally start by walking for one minute and running for one minute for about ten minutes. Gradually increase how long you run for and decrease how long you walk for. Over several weeks you will build up to 5 km and what an achievement that will be!
- Don't compare yourself with other people. This is not about them, it's about you. Your values are what count here so do what's important to you.
- Give yourself a break. No plan works perfectly. Things will go wrong for all sorts of reasons so give yourself a break if that happens.
- Do something for someone else. This could be someone you already know or a complete stranger. Activities that are good for other people have a double bonus. Think about doing some voluntary work that fits with one of your values. It doesn't need to take long or be difficult.

If you managed to read parts of this chapter or even the whole chapter then well done! Maybe you even had a go at filling in some of the logs? That's great but don't worry if you haven't done it yet. You might find that you come up with some ideas later on.

TAKE-HOME MESSAGES

Feeling depressed can make you less active and being less active can make you even more depressed. It's easy to get stuck in this unhelpful cycle when you are low. Finding activities in the areas that you value most in your life will help you to break out of this cycle. The more you take part in these activities, the more able you will be to overcome low mood and depression.

9

Thoughts on trial

Feeling low and depressed comes with lots of other problems, and these often add to depression and make us feel even worse. In the last chapter we looked at the problem of inactivity and at ways of becoming more active. In this chapter we are going to focus on our thoughts. Thoughts are tricky things. They come and go all the time but we are often not even aware of them. This means that they can sneak in and make us feel bad without us even noticing them.

In this chapter we will:

- Show how thoughts can lead to depression and keep us depressed.
- Identify common thinking traps.
- Help you catch your thoughts.
- Identify your thinking traps.
- Put your thinking traps on trial – are they reasonable?
- Develop and strengthen helpful thoughts.
- Learn how to ignore or let go of 'stuck' thoughts.

How do thoughts lead to depression and keep us depressed?

If you are depressed and low you probably have a lot of negative thoughts about a wide range of different things including yourself, the world and the future.

What do we mean by thoughts? Thoughts include all kinds of things that enter our minds. We remember things in the past, make plans for the future, try to work out what other people think about us and try to solve problems, all inside our heads.

Sometimes our thoughts are in words, we are almost talking inside our heads:

'What if he/she doesn't like me?'

'What shall I wear?'

'What shall I do at the weekend?'

'I really like him/her.'

Sometimes our thoughts are more like pictures in our heads – for example, a dress, a person's face, or a place we've visited can all be brought into our 'mind's eye'.

Our thoughts can also be linked to other senses – sounds, music and smells can all be part of our thoughts. When our thoughts include pictures, sounds, smells, taste or touch we call these 'images'.

A really powerful thought might include a combination of pictures, smells and sounds. So, for example, try to bring to mind a time when you went to the park in the summer. Perhaps close your eyes. Let the images come into your mind. Who else was there, what was the weather like, what food did you have to eat?

If you spend a bit of time on the memory a whole range of thoughts about it might come to mind – the smell of grass, the texture of the grass against your hand, the size, shape and colour of the trees, or the picnic rug, the faces of the people you were with, the sound of an ice-cream van or children playing in the background, the taste of the soggy sandwiches in your mouth. The more different ways we have of remembering things the stronger and more real they can feel.

How do thoughts make us feel bad?

1. Thoughts are powerful and can change how we feel

Powerful thoughts are often linked with feelings and emotions. Our thoughts are not linked to any specific time or place. Sometimes they are linked to memories and these can be happy memories and unhappy memories. Our thoughts also include the future – we have the ability to look into the future and to use our imagination to think about things that haven't even happened yet.

Imagine this situation. It's Saturday morning. You hear the postman at the door. On the doormat is a yellow envelope addressed to you. Your name and address are printed on a white sticker so you can't tell who it's from. You open it up and it's an invitation from an old friend you haven't seen for about a year. They are having a party in three weeks.

What does that make you think? Let's look at some of the options

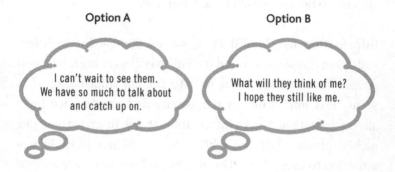

Straight away we can see that these thoughts could make us feel very differently. Thought A is likely to lead to feeling excited and happy. Thought B makes us feel a little bit worried and a bit anxious.

In this situation, what we think can have a direct effect on our mood and feelings. Can you think of any other thoughts that you could have in this situation? What would those thoughts make you feel?

Because our thoughts can be so varied and so creative, almost every situation can be thought about in a different way. And these different ways can lead to lots of different kinds of feelings.

2. Thoughts help us make sense of the world

Two important facts about the world we live in mean that we all have to take shortcuts in our thinking.

Information overload!!! First, we are bombarded by information in the world around us. This has always been true and people have evolved to be able to cut out information that seems less important. In the twenty-first century we have almost infinite access to information at our fingertips via our mobile phones, PCs and tablets. We could not possibly pay attention to everything. This means we have to ignore a lot of things completely. We also have to make a lot of quick decisions about all the information around us. We take shortcuts to get through the overload.

Caution! The world is full of unclear information! Second, all the information around us is a little bit unclear. This is true of lots of things in the world. When something is unclear we have to work harder to understand what it means and it is easy to make mistakes.

How do we use shortcuts when we think?

Read these words out loud. As you do, think about the meaning of each word and try to picture the word in your mind. Or put the word into a sentence so that it makes sense.

Sink / Bed / Bark / Mummy / Rock / Shoot

Do you know what those words have in common?

Every one of them has at least two different meanings (which makes them homonyms); they look the same and they sound the same but they mean something different. Without more context or information you can't tell which meaning is intended. Some of them (e.g. sink, shoot) have a meaning which is more negative than the other meaning. Did you notice that when you read them out?

What picture did you see when you read out the word 'sink'? How about the sentence you made up to include the word 'sink'? Did you visualize a place to do the washing up or brush your teeth, or did you visualize a ship sinking in the water?

If you want to test yourself, see how many words with double meanings you can think of and compare them with our list on p. 226.

How do you use shortcuts?

What's really interesting is that your mood can influence how your mind 'reads' each word. People who are depressed or worried are more likely to visualize a boat sinking rather than a place to do the washing up (sink), and a gun rather than part of a plant (shoot).

In contrast, people who are not depressed have a tendency to see things as less negative or more positive. So if they read those words out loud they would probably 'see' a place to do the washing up (sink) and a plant or flower (shoot). A real-life example of this is that most people (about 75 per cent) think that they are an above-average driver. Is this possible? Obviously not – lots of people must be wearing rose-tinted glasses when they imagine themselves driving.

Psychologists call this tendency to take something unclear and to lean towards seeing it as negative or positive as a **thinking bias.** It is completely normal to have a thinking bias – this is just a tendency to lean one way or another in our thinking – towards the positive, or the negative. It's as if some people are looking at the world through a pair of brown- or grey-tinted glasses and other people are looking at the world through a pair of rose-tinted glasses.

Here's a very well-known kind of thinking bias:

Is the glass half full? Or is the glass half empty? Obviously it could be either – neither bias is 'right' or 'wrong' they are just taking a different perspective.

There are a lot of different kinds of thinking biases:

Memory: We can have a bias to remember happy or unhappy memories. What do you think we are more likely to remember when we are depressed – good times or bad times? Yep, it's bad times. When we are depressed bad memories come quicker to mind and are easier to remember than happy memories. This means that we are more likely to be flooded with unhappy times from the past, which can make us feel even worse.

Attention: Stop for a minute and pay attention to what is going on around you. Just wait and listen. What information are your senses picking up? What can you hear? What can you see?

Depending on where you are as you read this (e.g. at home, on a bus, in a park) the world around you will be very different. You might be able to hear the radio, traffic, people talking, music playing, birds singing, or dogs barking, or all of these things at the same time. All of these different things give us information but most of the time we don't notice it. We are good at switching off our attention and directing it to specific things.

Perhaps you won't be surprised that people who are feeling depressed and low are more likely to pay attention to things in the world that remind them of bad things. Can you think of ways in which you do this?

Imagine if you were frightened of dogs. In the park what do you think you would pay most attention to? Probably dogs.

You'd probably notice **all** the dogs. You'd notice if the dogs were on leads or not, how close they were, if they were running towards you and how big they were. And while you were checking all the dogs and making sure that they didn't get too close to you, do you think you would enjoy being in the park? Would you be able to pay attention to what your friends were saying? Would you enjoy their jokes? Would you be able to join in properly? It's unlikely.

So what we notice and what we pay attention to directly affects how we feel. Also, when we pay attention to certain things we ignore a lot of other things. So if we tend to notice more negative things, this will increase how sad and unhappy we feel, and it means we don't take notice of positive things that could help us feel better.

3. Thoughts are sneaky and hard to notice

You are thinking almost all of the time. But how often do you notice your thoughts? Probably not very often. Our thoughts are just like background music – we can tune in to them and pay attention, but we often don't.

This wouldn't matter if our thoughts are usually quite positive, or are usually neutral. The effect on our mood would be good or wouldn't matter. But if our thoughts tend to be more negative this can have a huge impact on our mood and feelings. We would not notice this but it would be happening all the time, every day.

And because our thoughts, feelings and behaviour are all connected (remember the hot cross bun?), sneaky negative thoughts also change our behaviour. So without even noticing it we can get stuck in a negative cycle, a thinking trap.

4. Thoughts can snowball – a small negative thought can quickly become a big negative thought

Let's use the party invitation example again.

'What will they think of me? I hope they still like me.'

This thought doesn't sound very negative. Maybe it makes us feel a little bit worried and anxious. But if we are low and unhappy it can quickly grow. Let's look at how that might happen – what thoughts might follow the first?

- 'What will they think of me? I hope they still like me.'
- 'What shall I wear?'
- 'I've got nothing to wear!'
- 'I'll feel stupid and ugly.'
- 'I'm not very good at talking to people.'
- 'I'll be really embarrassed and uncomfortable.'
- 'It'll be awful, no one will speak to me.'
- 'They'll think I'm really stupid and ugly.'
- 'They'll be sorry they invited me.'
- 'It'll be better not to go at all.'
- 'That's it; I'm not going.'
- 'If I don't go it just shows how useless I am.'
- 'I'll never make any friends.'
- 'I'll always be lonely.'
- 'Why do I always mess everything up?'

It's scary really how quickly our negative thoughts can grow. They are a bit like a snowball rolling down a hill, getting quicker and quicker, and bigger and bigger.

Putting thoughts on trial

OK, so we know a few things about how thoughts lead to depression and keep it going:

1. The world is full of information that is not clear.

2. We all use shortcuts to deal with the overload.

3. Shortcuts can lead to thinking 'traps'.

4. If we feel low we are more likely to fall into a negative trap.

5. We probably won't notice that it's a trap.

6. A negative trap will make us feel even worse.

Here's an example of a thinking trap that Emily found herself in. The situation here is that Emily saw her friend Christy talking to the girls who had bullied her.

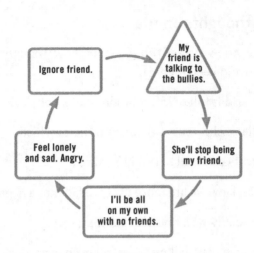

Because Emily saw Christy talking to the girls who had been mean to her she immediately *thought the worst.* She *assumed* that Christy would stop being her friend. She *imagined* herself with no friends at all. She believed these thoughts and could even 'see' in her mind the future that she predicted, alone, with no friends. But Emily didn't have any real reason to think these things. She didn't have any evidence that Christy would stop being her friend.

Emily's thoughts made her feel even more lonely and sad. She also felt upset with Christy and a bit angry with her. So instead of talking to Christy and being friendly, she ignored her. This confused Christy. Do you think it was likely to improve their friendship? Probably not. It might even have made their friendship a little bit worse.

It's understandable that Emily thought the worst. But how helpful was it?

Are there other, more helpful thoughts she could have had?

Escape the thinking trap

How can we get out of the thinking trap? We're going to make some suggestions to help you put your thoughts on trial. It might take a bit of practice to be able to do this. Don't worry – everyone finds it hard. We just aren't very used to paying attention to our thoughts and so they just sneak past us.

There are four stages:

1. Catch the thought – you have to catch them before you can do anything with them.

2. Check the thought – is there a trap in there? We'll tell you about a few of the most common thinking traps – it's likely you'll recognize one or two of them.

3. Test the thought – is it reasonable? Or is it just a negative trap?

4. Challenge and replace negative thoughts with more helpful thoughts.

Catching thoughts

This is probably the most difficult bit of putting our thoughts on trial. Thoughts are like habits – they become a bit automatic and happen without us noticing. Emily's thoughts about Christy were so quick to happen that she didn't even notice them. What she did notice was how sad and lonely she felt. And what she did was to ignore Christy, something that probably made things even worse.

So how can we start to catch our thoughts? Usually it's easiest to start with a specific situation. Something that happened recently is best. It can help to write this down, to keep a record of it. Also, writing down situations and thoughts can be a helpful way of standing back and getting some distance from them.

Let's start with something that happened last week. Can you think of a time last week when something happened that made you feel bad?

On p. 219 there is a log for writing this down.

We'll also fill one in so that you can see how to do it. Our example is the party invitation we mentioned before.

What happened (the easy bit)

- Write down what you were doing and where you were.
- If it's relevant also add who you were with.

Time and date	What happened	What you thought How much you believe it	Feeling How strong is the feeling?
9.30 a.m. Saturday	Party invitation arrived in post		

Thoughts

- What went through your mind? What did you say to yourself? What did you 'see' in your mind's eye?
- Write down your thoughts. You might be able to catch more than one – if so, great, put them all down. (We've only put down a few to give you the idea.)
- How much do you believe each thought? Rate the thought(s) from zero – don't believe it at all to 100 – completely believe it.

Time and date	What happened	What you thought How much you believe it	Feeling How strong is the feeling?
9.30 a.m. Saturday	Party invitation arrived in post	What will they think of me? I hope they still like me. 50 per cent	
		It'll be awful, no one will speak to me. 70 per cent	
		Why do I always mess everything up? 100 per cent	

Feeling

- How did that make you feel? Good or bad?
- Can you describe it a bit more? For example, if it was bad, were you sad, worried, angry, upset, irritable or a mixture of these? If you had more than one feeling, write them all down.
- How strong was the feeling? Or if you had more than one, how strong was each one?
- Rate the feeling from zero – nothing at all to 100 – maximum possible strength.

Time and date	What happened	What you thought How much you believe it	Feeling How strong is the feeling?
9.30 a.m. Saturday	Party invitation arrived in post	What will they think of me? I hope they still like me. 50 per cent	Worried Anxious 80 per cent
		I'll be awful. No one will speak to me. 70 per cent	Left out Sad 90 per cent
		Why do I always mess everything up? 100 per cent	Useless Depressed 100 per cent

OK, how was that? Can you think of more than one example from the past week? You might find that your activity log gives you some clues as to times when you felt low, and it might remind you of where you were and what you were doing.

If you find it difficult to remember things that happened last week, don't worry. You can start now by using the next few things that happen that trigger an unhappy, sad, angry, irritable or worried feeling. At this stage don't worry about getting it right or wrong. You can always try again.

My thought-catching log

Time and date	Situation – what happened	What you thought How much you believe it	Feeling How strong is the feeling?

Check your thoughts

When you are able to catch your thoughts you can start to put them on trial. There are a lot of ways we can make mistakes in our thinking. **We think of these as common thinking traps**.

Thinking traps are not always unhelpful. We can fall into positive traps as well and they probably make us feel better.

Remember how most of us think we are much better than aver-age drivers? We know that can't be true. That's us wearing our rose-tinted glasses!

When we have thinking traps that keep us feeling unhappy and depressed, or make us feel even worse, or lead to us behaving in ways that make things worse, it's time to catch them, check them, challenge them and chuck them out.

Here are some of the most common thinking traps. We've given you a few examples, but can you find any examples from your own life? Your thought-catching log might include a few. We've left a space for you to add some examples of your own.

Black and white thinking (or all or nothing thinking)

'I *must* make a good impression at this party or I'll *never* make friends.'

'If I don't get an A in the exam it'll prove how stupid I am.'

.... (Your example)

Over-generalizing

'She's cross with me; I know that she hates me, everyone hates me.'

'If she doesn't invite me to her party I'll *never* make any new friends.'

.... (Your example)

Predicting the worst

'I'm bound to fail that exam. My life will be ruined. I'll never get to college, or get a good job.'

'I'll hate that party; no one will speak to me.'

'She'll stop being my friend.'

.... (Your example)

Self-blaming

'It's because I'm stupid/ugly/horrible/unloveable.'

'I've let everyone down.'

.... (Your example)

Mind reading

'She'll think I'm stupid.'

'They all think I'm ugly.'

'My parents will be so disappointed in me.'

.... (Your example)

Jumping to conclusions

'If I don't get picked for the team I'll be so embarrassed, I won't be able to play again.'

'Where are they? They're late. They're not coming. I've been stood up.'

'They're whispering. I bet they're talking about me.'

.... (Your example)

Challenging your thoughts

Putting your thoughts on trial

This is the tricky bit. You are going to check if you can rely on your thoughts. Are they fair, or are they a bit biased? If they are biased you might be looking at the world through brown- or grey-tinted glasses? Maybe this is making things look worse than they really are.

A good starting point is to remember that just because you have a thought, it doesn't mean it is true. It could be true, it could be partly true, or it could be completely wrong. Life is not as black and white as we sometimes think. Life is full of grey, somewhere between black and white and harder to notice.

Let's look again at one of Emily's thoughts:

'She'll stop being my friend.'

Does Emily know that is true? No. Is it inevitable that Christy will stop being her friend? No. Does Emily have much evidence for that thought? Probably not.

How would your thoughts stand up to such questioning? If you put your thoughts on trial how would they do? Some questions you can use to test your thoughts and put them on trial include:

- What's the evidence for that thought?

- Do I have enough information to draw that conclusion?

- How could I get more information?

- Is there another way of thinking about that?

- How reasonable was that thought?

- If my best friend had that thought what would I say to them?

- What other thoughts could I have about that?

- Can you imagine what someone else might think if they were in that situation?

That might seem a little bit vague so let's use the party invitation again. We've seen how one little thought seemed to lead to a whole string of negative thoughts. Let's look at each one of them and see if we can find any thinking errors:

You are invited to a PARTY

What will they think of me? I hope they still like me.

Thought	Thinking trap
'What will they think of me? I hope they still like me?'	Not too negative – could be neutral. If you go you'll find out.
'What shall I wear?'	Good question, you could make a plan.
'I've got *nothing* to wear!'	Is that actually true? Is this black and white thinking? There's still time to get something new.
'I'll feel stupid and ugly.'	You are predicting the worst. Do you actually *know* what you will feel? Just because you think it doesn't make it true.
'I'm not very good at talking to people.'	Is this true? What evidence do you have? What would your best friend say to you about this? Have there been times when you managed to talk to others? If you are not very good at talking to people is this a skill that you could practise? How do other people who find it difficult to talk to other people manage? Could you practise listening instead?

'I'll be really embarrassed and uncomfortable.'	Sounds like you are predicting the worst again.
	Do you really know how you will feel in three weeks' time?
	What other feelings are possible?
'It'll be awful, no one will speak to me.'	Now you are *'awful-izing'* (and yes, we made that word up!).
	How do you know what will happen at the party?
	Just because you think something does that make it true?
	If no one spoke to you what could you do about that?
'They will think I'm really stupid and ugly.'	Will they? How do you know? Are you making the mistake of mind reading?
'They'll be sorry they invited me.'	This is definitely mind reading. Face it, you don't have super powers.
'It'll be better not to go at all.'	Based on what?
	Is your mind reading, predicting the worst, and black and white thinking helping you to make the right decisions?
	Have you worried about something similar in the past and you found that it turned out OK when you went?

Finding more helpful thoughts

So you have caught your thoughts, checked and had a good look at them, put them on trial and found that many of them are full of traps. What now? Next we replace the automatic thoughts with an alternative thought. We're looking for something that is a bit more neutral, a bit more balanced and a bit more accurate.

This does not mean that you have to replace a negative thought with a positive thought. Remember, the world is not black and white; it's also grey. So alternative thoughts do not have to be upbeat and 'cheerleaderly' (this is another word we made up, hopefully you get what we mean). The aim here is to be more balanced and to shift your thinking habits away from being always negative.

Situation: At home, alone, party invitation

Thought	Feeling How strong?	New, more helpful thought	Feeling How strong?
'What will they think of me?' 'I hope they still like me?'	Worried, anxious. 80 per cent	'They wouldn't invite me if they didn't like me.'	Worried, anxious. 60 per cent
		'It might be nice to see them again.'	Pleased. 40 per cent

'I've got nothing to wear.'	Fed up. 70 per cent	'I'll go and check my wardrobe.' 'I can go and buy something for the party.'	OK 50 per cent Relieved 80 per cent
'I'll feel stupid and ugly.' 'I'll be really embarrassed and uncom- fortable.'	Sad. 80 per cent	'How do I know what I'll feel like?' 'It's too early to know.'	Sad. 60 per cent
'I'm not very good at talking to people.'	Useless. 100 per cent	'Some people do seem better at talking to other people than me.' 'Can I practise talking to people I don't know?'	Useless. 80 per cent Good idea. 60 per cent
'They will think I'm really stupid and ugly.'	Lonely. 90 per cent	'How do I know that's true?' 'They wouldn't invite me if they didn't want to see me.'	Lonely. 10 per cent

Like any thoughts, your new, more helpful thoughts might not always be 'true'. The aim is to find a more balanced thought that is not part of a negative trap. Remember, *all* thoughts are just thoughts. Thoughts are not facts.

It's also important to rate your feelings again after you consider the new, more helpful thought. In the example above, you'll see that your feelings won't necessary change completely but gradually you might see a shift in your mood and feelings.

This is a new skill that you are learning. As we said before, it's not easy. Like any skills it is important to practise. As you know, with practise things will get easier. As you practise you will learn about yourself and about the kind of thinking traps you use most often. You will see how your thinking traps make you feel more sad and unhappy. You will also start to check your thoughts more often, in real life.

When you start to check your thoughts in real life you are able to change them to more helpful thoughts. That is fantastic. After a while the more helpful thoughts will become a new habit. This is a habit we want you to keep.

Here is a form to record your own thoughts, feelings and new, more helpful thoughts. See how you get on.

Thoughts on trial

Situation _____

Thought	Feeling How strong? 0–100 per cent	New, more helpful thought	Feeling How strong? 0–100 per cent

Dealing with 'stuck thoughts'

Sometimes it's hard to challenge thoughts – some thoughts go round and round in our heads and get stuck. Sometimes we try to work through a problem and go over and over the same thing. You may recall that this is called **rumination** and it is a common symptom of depression.

It can be hard to recognize that you are stuck in your thinking. This is because we often try to think through our problems and believe that if we just think hard enough we will figure a way through them. Some kinds of thinking through problems can be useful. We can work out how to avoid problems in the future or take the time to see things from someone else's point of view. This is a way of solving problems.

But at other times, thinking things over is not helpful and doesn't get us anywhere. A specific kind of rumination is called **brooding**. Thinking about what went wrong in the past and focusing on what has already happened can become brooding and can make you feel worse. If you find you are asking yourself the following questions over and over, or have these thoughts going round and round in your head, you might be brooding.

- 'Why on earth did I do it that way?'
- 'Would it have made any difference if I'd done it differently?'
- 'How did I get myself into that situation?'
- 'I should have said "........". Then if they said "........", maybe that would have worked?'
- 'Why does this kind of thing always happen to me?'
- 'What have I done wrong?'

- 'Is it something about the kind of person I am?'
- 'Do I deserve to have bad things happen to me?'

If you find yourself asking these sorts of questions and you are not getting anywhere you are stuck. Doing more and more of the same kind of thinking is not going to help. Chewing over the same questions with your friends and family probably won't help either. Here are some ways to stop ruminating and start getting on with life.

1. Distract yourself

This is so simple it's hard to believe it can work. But really, it can.

You've seen distraction work with little children – you might have done it yourself if you are babysitting or have younger brothers or sisters. Or you might do it yourself with your parents – if you distract them when they are about to ask you a tricky question it can work wonders.

So how can you distract yourself?

- Exercise is good. If you are putting effort into running, cycling, dance, an aerobics class or a game of football you can't pay attention to your 'stuck' thoughts at the same time.
- Watch a film, play music, read a novel – get lost in something outside of yourself.
- Do something practical. This is also good if it's helping

someone else. For example, cooking dinner for your family, making a cake, hanging out some washing, cleaning the bathroom, or playing with younger brothers or sisters can be good ways of distracting yourself.

- Play a computer game, preferably one that's quite hard!
- Learn how to knit or sew or do DIY.
- Visit a sick or elderly relative or neighbour; talk to them about their life and feelings.

What other ways could you use to distract yourself?

2. Try problem solving

There is a whole chapter on problem solving so have a look at ways to tackle your thoughts in a constructive way. Have a look at Chapter 11.

3. Learn to let your negative thoughts 'go'

This is a different way to deal with stuck thoughts. Remember thoughts are just thoughts. They come and go, in and out of mind. Some are positive and some are negative. Thoughts are not facts. Thoughts themselves are not real even if they are about things that were real. Much of the time we don't even notice our thoughts so we know that they can come and go. Have a look at Chapter 12 at the end of the book for more on this.

Often thoughts that get stuck are about things that happened in the past. It can be something that happened a long time ago or earlier today. Things in the past can't be changed. You can learn from the past and this is important. But if you find yourself thinking about the same thing that you cannot possibly change it's probably time to let it go. Even though you can't change what's happened in your past, you can change how you feel about it and how you let it affect your future.

Bad memories and thoughts can be caught up with a lot of difficult feelings like anger and rage, loss and failure. If this is the case for you, those memories and the experiences that went with them are part of who you are. But only *a part* of who you are. Your past experiences do not define who you are or what you can become. This is why accepting the past and focusing on what is happening now and in the future can be a much more creative way forward. Have a look at your life values and goals to remind yourself of your future.

Stuck thoughts can also include a lot of self-blame. Do you have a critical voice inside your own head? Are you your own worst critic? If you find yourself beating yourself up for the mistakes you've made it is time to give yourself a break. Just as it is important to be tolerant and compassionate towards other people, we need to be tolerant and compassionate towards ourselves. Just as we try to be kind and thoughtful to our friends, so we need to be kind and thoughtful to ourselves (see Chapter 12).

You can read more about why it is important to be compassionate and kind to yourself here: www.compassionatemind.co.uk.

Other ways to escape from stuck thinking

1. Writing about bad experiences can help you to deal with the jumbled-up thoughts and feelings. Don't worry about your writing or getting every last bit right. Just get it down on paper. Don't write it for anyone else – you can simply put it away in a drawer. This is just for you.

2. Allocate a specific worry time each day. Give yourself thirty minutes for any worrying and make sure you are busy for the rest of the day. If worries and stuck thoughts start outside of this time you know you can put them aside and come back to them later during the worry time.

3. If bad thoughts are intruding into your mind during the day and getting in the way of your life it can be helpful to talk them through with someone else. This could be a parent or other relative, a teacher, sports coach or school counsellor. If you don't think you can talk about it to someone you know, what about using a telephone or online help? See p. 47 for contact details for online and telephone support services which are specifically for young people.

4. Try mindfulness meditation. Mindfulness meditation is a way of dealing with difficult feelings, and has been shown to help with depression and low mood. Mindfulness helps you to pay attention to what is happening now, rather than thinking about and worrying about the past or the future. You can learn about mindfulness in lots of different places and in different ways. Some schools include mindfulness teaching. Your GP might be able to refer you to a

mindfulness group where you can learn with other people. We have included some more information about mindfulness below and in Chapter 12.

Want to know more?

www.mindful.org

This is a UK-based organization that provides online counselling and support for young people.

www.studentsagainstdepression.org

Students against depression who also tweet and blog. They work directly with colleges and universities.

www.respectyourself.org.uk

A website for young people. You can be emailed daily messages that focus on your strengths and your future.

www.bemindful.co.uk

You can find out more about mindfulness here. There are also websites specifically for young people who are interested in mindfulness, for example:

www.mindfulyouth.org

Information about mindfulness and mindfulness training for young people.

Common homonyms – did you find more?

Bat / Bank / Fair / Fine / Spot / Lie / Light / Right / Mean /
Fly / Pound / Pole / Race / Watch / Rig / Tip / Trip

Additional worksheets

You can find useful handouts for this and the other chapters on the following websites:

Youth Space

www.youthspace.me/resources

Cognitive behaviour therapy self-help resources

www.getselfhelp.co.uk/freedownloads2.htm

TAKE-HOME MESSAGES

Negative thinking patterns and common thinking traps can lead to feelings of depression. If we are able to catch our thoughts, identify any thinking traps and put our thoughts on trial, we can decide whether the way we are thinking is realistic and helpful. We can then develop more helpful ways of thinking in order to feel better.

10

Testing things out – getting the facts

In this chapter we want to introduce the idea of **behaviour experiments** or **fact finders**.

What's a fact finder?

Fact finders can help us to work out whether we are missing anything in the way we think about certain things. We can put something to the test to get all the facts and check if it works the way we thought. Fact finders are especially helpful when we are feeling low or worried. This is because when we feel low or worried we often see the world through brown- or grey-tinted lenses. You may recall from the previous chapter that just because we think something, it doesn't mean it's actually true. Depression can often mean we are caught in a thinking trap. Fact finders help us to figure out whether our way of thinking about something is based on reality or not.

So, for example, someone called Jerry might think that all cats are horrible and evil. Jerry has never actually had a cat and he hasn't ever spent any time with cats. Maybe this is a belief that he just picked up from his family because someone in the family has always hated cats. Every time he sees a cat he tries to avoid it and he avoids going over to his friend's house because his friend has a cat. Anyway, one day Jerry decides that he wants to put this thought to the test to see if it is actually 100 per cent true.

Can you think of any fact finders for the thought that all cats are horrible and evil?

1. Jerry could do a survey and ask his friends and other people he knows what they think of cats. Then he could add up the number of people who said that cats are horrible and evil. He could compare it with the number of people who felt differently about cats.

228

2. He could find a way of spending some time with cats to see what they are really like. Maybe he could ask a friend who has a cat whether he could go over and feed it a few times.

3. He could do some research about cats to understand a bit more about them and see what cat owners and experts say about cats.

You get the idea.

It would be interesting to see what Jerry found out through these fact finders.

In Jerry's case you might agree that there's probably a big chance that he may find many people who really like cats (some who even love them). He might also find out some interesting facts about cats and their behaviour, which might not fit in with the idea that they are all evil. He might even find that spending time with his friend's cat was OK, maybe even nice because the cat is very affectionate and playful.

So these fact finders might then actually lead Jerry to change his mind about cats. Rather than thinking that all cats are horrible and evil, he might think instead that cats can be interesting, some people really like them and some cats seem to be OK.

This is what we might call a **balanced view**. It means that rather than only thinking one way about something, through the use of fact finders, Jerry has been able to come up with a view that's based on lots of facts.

Having a more balanced view helps Jerry because he no longer avoids cats and places where they might be. It's not like he loves them or wants one himself, it's just that it no longer makes any difference to where he wants to go and how he feels.

So in this example the fact finders helped to change Jerry's views and behaviour and made his life a bit easier.

Setting up your own fact finders

- The best way to plan fact finders is firstly to write down the **thoughts or beliefs** that you want to test.
- Next you write down an idea for the **fact finder** to test these out.
- Then you write down your **prediction** about what you think is going to happen when you do the test.
- Then you **do it**.
- Next you note down **what actually happened** and **whether the prediction was right**.
- Finally, whatever the outcome, it's helpful to have a think about **what the outcome means** in relation to the thought(s) being tested. Is there a more **balanced view**?

Let's think about Robert, Lin and Emily.

Are there any fact finders that could help them to get more facts about something?

Robert has the thought that 'none of my friends care about me and spending time with them will make me feel worse'. This thought makes him feel lonely, sad and angry. How could he test this thought out?

_____

_____

_____

_____

_____

_____

Lin thinks that she needs to rest and sleep as much as possible in order to feel less tired and that doing too much and sleeping less will make her feel worse. What's a good fact finder for Lin's thoughts?

_____

_____

_____

_____

_____

_____

_____

Emily thinks that everyone hates her at school and they all think she's a freak. This is making her very upset and is making it very difficult for her to go to school. Could there be a way to test out these thoughts?

_____

_____

_____

_____

_____

_____

BUT WHAT IF FACT FINDERS TELL US WE WERE RIGHT?

You might be wondering what if sometimes we test something out and we find out that the way we were thinking about it was actually true.

What then?

Well, first of all it's handy to know that the way we were thinking about something was actually correct and it wasn't just us missing something important.

Second, when you have all the facts you are then in a much better position to do something about the issue. It's much harder to try to solve things when you don't have all the facts!

We will return to this later in Chapter 11.

Robert's fact finder

Thought(s) to test

Robert has thoughts that none of his friends care about him or want to see him and that spending time with them will make him feel worse. He tries to come up with a fact finder for this.

Fact finder

He decides to text three of his friends who he used to play football with to see if he can hang out with them one afternoon.

Prediction

Robert predicts that none of his friends will bother texting him back and even if they do they won't want to hang out with him. He also predicts that even if he does hang out with them, it won't make him feel any better or maybe even make him feel worse.

Do it

Robert decides to do this on a Friday afternoon, when he is feeling more relaxed. He sends a text to his three friends saying 'Hi, it's Rob, what u up to?' He then waits to see what happens.

So what happened?

Ten minutes after Robert sent his text one of his friends replies that he is bored. An hour later his other friend says he's going out tonight and asks if Robert wants to come. The third friend doesn't text back and this makes Robert wonder whether this whole tester was worth the trouble. Robert decides not to go out that night with one of his friends, but they agree to meet up the following day at the park on the football field.

The next day Robert goes to the park, although he is not feeling great and he just wants to stay in his room. When he gets there he sees his other friend (the one who didn't text back). It turns out that one of the other guys told him they were meeting up and so he decided to come too.

Robert suddenly remembers that this friend is completely hopeless when it comes to sending texts; he never used to do it much before. The others come eventually and one of them has brought a football.

Robert is quite nervous to start with. It has been so long since he has played football, he's worried he'll be rubbish. They start kicking the ball around. After a while a few other boys from school join them and they decide to have a game. They end up playing for about an hour.

While he's playing football Robert doesn't think much about anything except the game. He notices that he is not feeling bad. In fact he is feeling quite good, really alive. After the game they buy some soft drinks and snacks, and hang out nearby just talking and eating. Robert heads home after this.

Was the prediction right?

No, the prediction was not right at all.

First of all, Robert's friends all seemed to want to meet up with him or at least they all wanted to meet up together.

Secondly, hanging out with them didn't make Robert feel worse, it actually made him feel much better for a while.

What does it all mean?

Robert found out that his predictions were not right. It is possible that because he is feeling low and unhappy he expects the worst to happen.

Is there a balanced view?

The balanced view might be something like this, 'Some of my friends seem to want to hang out with me so maybe they care. Spending time with them can make me feel better.'

What's next?

Robert thinks about seeing his friends again in a few days. He remembers how much he used to love playing football and wonders if he might play again soon.

Lin's fact finder

Thought(s) to test

Lin thinks that sleeping and resting less and doing more will make her feel more tired and she will feel worse.

Fact finder

After reading Chapter 8 (Feeling and Doing), Lin decided to test this out by planning to do more on one Saturday. This was really hard for her because she didn't feel like doing anything. She wanted to stay in her room on her own.

She makes an agreement with herself to give this a go and just see what happens. She decides that she can stay in her room and rest more on Sunday.

So she makes a short list of activities to do on Saturday. She makes sure that some of these activities are things she used to like doing before she started to feel so bad.

Here's her list:

1. Get up at 9 a.m. and don't go back to bed.
2. Have a proper breakfast downstairs.
3. Go shopping with Mum.
4. Go for a walk and take my sketchpad with me.
5. Look on the Internet for some local dance classes and see when the next sessions are starting.
6. Make a cake.
7. Spend the evening with my family watching TV.

Lin knows that she will need to talk to her mum about some of these activities. She needs to ask if they can both go shopping and if it is OK to bake a cake in the afternoon.

She tells her mum that she is doing this and her mum seems pleased. Lin looks at her list and feels a bit overwhelmed. It's so much more than she usually does on a Saturday. She decides that she won't make herself do anything she doesn't want to do and if she only wants to do one or two things on this list on the day then that's OK. She's just going to see how it feels one bit at a time.

Prediction

Lin predicts that it's going to be really hard and she will just feel worse as the day goes on, and will feel more and more tired.

Do it

Saturday comes. Lin had set her alarm clock for 9 a.m. but it was very hard to get up. She forces herself to do it and feels really tired. Lin goes downstairs and has some breakfast with the family. Her mum reminds her that they can go shopping in an hour. Lin forces herself to eat the breakfast, she's not really hungry. She starts to think that this is all too hard. Lin goes upstairs and resists going to bed but instead picks out her clothes for the shopping trip and goes to have a shower.

So what happened?

By the time they leave for the shopping trip Lin feels more awake and a tiny bit better. She and her mum go shopping. At times it's really boring but she also has a chance to look at some nice clothes with Mum and they have a chat like they haven't for a while. Mum gets her a muffin and they sit and have a cup of tea in a coffee shop. Mum tells Lin that she's glad she decided to come out with her.

Lin gets back home and notices that she is a bit tired but not like she was expecting. Lin decides to go for a walk as planned. She takes her sketchpad and finds a spot where she can sit and make a quick sketch of a tree. It's not too bad.

Lin gets back home and wonders if she has enough energy to do the other things on her list. She decides to try the next thing to see how she feels. She doesn't really feel like baking because she feels she will just make a mess of it. Her mum reminds her about this activity and helps her get all the items out ready. Lin very reluctantly starts to get it all ready. Ten minutes later she is putting all the ingredients together and is actually enjoying herself, much to her surprise. She puts the cake in the oven and starts clearing up. She snacks on the chocolate icing as she puts the finishing touches to the cake.

Making the cake takes longer than she expected so Lin decides not to look at dance classes on the Internet, but after tea she spends some of the evening with her family watching TV. When her cake is ready everyone has a piece. They all seem to like it and Lin is pleased with the taste as well. They watch a funny film and then Lin decides to go to her room for an hour before bed. Lin looks at her list and is really pleased with how much she managed to do today.

Was the prediction right?

No. Lin concludes that rather than feeling more tired, the day has made her feel a bit less tired in a way. This doesn't make sense to Lin because she was convinced it would be the other way around.

What does it all mean?

The fact finder has helped Lin to see that doing more, especially things that she used to enjoy, seems to give her more energy rather than less.

Is there a balanced view?

Lin decides that her balanced view goes something like this, 'Sleeping and resting is important but doing too much of this actually makes me more tired. Doing things I like seems to make me feel less tired sometimes.'

What's next?

Lin wants to repeat the tester on other days and with other activities to see how it makes her feel and whether it works again. She talks to her mum and they plan a list of activities for the next weekend.

Emily's fact finder

Thought(s) to test

Emily thinks that her friends are slowly turning against her and they are becoming friends with the people who bully her.

Fact finder

Ask her best friend Christy whether she and the other girls like the bullies.

Prediction

Emily thinks that Christy will tell her that she does like them and that she should try and be friends with them too.

Do it

Emily talks to Christy the following day at lunchtime.

So what happened?

Christy says that she doesn't like the bullies but that their other two friends do. She also says that the others are starting to hang around with the bullies more.

Was the prediction right?

Half yes and half no. Emily's best friend doesn't like the bullies but their other friends do seem to want to be friends with them.

What does it all mean?

The fact finder has shown Emily that she was only half right. Most importantly, she found out that her best friend was not turning against her.

Is there a balanced view?

After the fact finder, Emily's balanced view was, 'Some of my friends seem to like the bullies but my best friend doesn't. At least I know that my best friend is not turning against me.'

What's next?

Emily starts to think about who her true friends are. She wonders whether there is anything she can do about her other friends who are starting to hang out with the bullies (see what Emily does about this in Chapter 11).

Now it's your turn to have a go at doing a fact finder. Can you think of any thoughts or beliefs that have been bothering you or making you feel down (you might want to have a look back at Chapter 9 to see if you noted down any negative thoughts)? Is it worth putting these thoughts to the test to see if they are thinking traps?

Coming up with ideas for fact finders can be tricky and sometimes it's really hard. It's fine if you can't come up with any ideas right away. Often a lot of people ask others to help them with this. Maybe you can see if your family has any ideas about useful things to test out. Maybe you can even find some ideas for your family to test out themselves!

My fact finder

Thought(s) to test
Fact finder

Prediction
Do it
So what happened?
Was the prediction right?

What does it all mean?

Is there a balanced view?

What's next?

TAKE-HOME MESSAGES

Sometimes we need more facts and information in order to see whether the way we are thinking about something is really true, or whether it is the depression that is making us think this way. Planning and carrying out fact finders helps us to put these thoughts and beliefs to the test. It's a way of getting the full picture.

11

Solving problems

Problems! Who needs them?

Are problems our friends or enemies? Imagine for a moment life without any problems at all. Every day everything is sorted and nothing ever comes up for us to work out. We go about our lives and it all just happens around us – we don't have to do a thing. Great, hey? Or is it? If we never had to stop and sort anything out then it's possible we wouldn't have to think or do much about anything. And if we didn't have to think or do much about anything then that's starting to sound a bit boring. And if everything was always worked out for us and nothing ever needed planning then we might stop learning, or having wishes and desires, and we might even ask ourselves why we need our thinking brains at all? Actually, life without any problems is starting to sound very boring indeed. Even animals in the wild encounter problems all the time that need to be worked out. A lion, for example, may try to solve the problem of how to approach a herd of deer in the best possible way so it's not seen by them.

So, problems are a natural part of life and they make life interesting

Sorting problems can be exciting, frustrating, daunting, worrying, stressful, interesting, useful, depressing . . . We can have all sorts of emotions when we are faced with problems that need to be sorted. Do you remember what influences how we feel? Yes, it is how we think about it. Remember how easily our thoughts can snowball so that they quickly become more and more negative, and more and more overwhelming? Here's a reminder of how that can happen.

Two people might be faced with a problem such as losing their maths homework.

One person (Person A) might think the following about problems in general:

'Problems are terrible, they happen to me all the time. I can't do much about what happens to me.'

This person may go on to think:

- 'Oh no, this is awful.'
- 'I'm always losing things.'
- 'I can't believe I've done this.'
- 'Now I'm never going to find it.'
- 'I'm going to get in loads of trouble.'
- 'It's hopeless.'
- 'I'm hopeless.'

It's likely that thinking this way will make the person feel irritated, worried, hopeless and low. This might mean that they don't even try to solve the problem. Because they don't know how to solve it, they try to avoid it.

The problem stays in the back of their mind though and keeps niggling at them. Every time they remember it, they feel even worse and try to avoid it even more. Guess what? The problem doesn't get solved and this person ends up feeling a bit useless and low. They also continue to think that having problems is terrible and that they don't know how to sort them out. Their confidence goes down.

Another person (Person B) may think this way about problems:

'Problems happen all the time to everyone.'

'They will happen to me too and usually they can be sorted one way or another.'

In the same situation as above, this may lead to other thoughts such as:

- 'OK, this is a bit of a pain but I can retrace my steps.'
- 'I'm sure I can work out where my homework is.'
- 'If not there's got to be something else I can do about it.'

This type of thinking will probably make the person feel OK, maybe a bit annoyed but also fairly hopeful that it can be sorted. These types of thoughts and feelings are likely to influence what the person does next. The person is more likely to try to come up with some solutions to the problem. Next they may try their solutions to see if they help and if not then try some other ones until the problem is solved. This makes the person feel that problems are not a huge deal, and many of them can be solved. This person ends up feeling OK about their ability to deal with tricky situations and their confidence goes up.

Actually, the bottom line is that sorting problems out makes us feel more confident and as a result, happier with ourselves. So the answer to the questions at the beginning of this chapter is that:

We all need problems, they're a part of life and make it interesting.

Problems are not our enemies, they're there to be solved and to help us learn and become more confident!

Keeping this attitude in mind towards problems helps us to be more like Person B.

So once we can remind ourselves of this positive attitude to problems, what's the next step? The next step is learning and practising how to solve problems. It's another skill that gets better and better the more we use it. It would be no good just to have a good attitude towards having problems and never get around to solving any. That would just be a waste and it wouldn't solve anything.

Solving problems vs rumination

When we have a problem we can sometimes get stuck in **dwelling** on the problem for too long. As we discussed before, this is known as rumination. Everyone does this from time to time but sometimes people get stuck turning the problem over and over in their minds for too long, and this makes them feel worse.

They might ask questions such as:

- 'Why is this happening?'
- 'Why am I having to deal with this?'
- 'What if I can't find a way out?'
- 'What is going to happen?'
- 'Why can't things be different?'

A much more helpful approach is to ask questions about **how** to solve this problem. Asking **how** questions leads to useful problem solving and means you are dealing with the issue, rather than turning it over and over in your mind.

Solving problems – step by step

This skill has particular steps that are best taken in the right order.

STEP 1 Decide on what the problem is – **name it:** 'The problem
is _____ '

STEP 2 Come up with some possible solutions – go on, add some funny and ridiculous ones too, it helps with imagination and ideas. You can ask a friend or family member to help. Get creative.

STEP 3 Think about each solution and how good you think it is – will it solve the problem completely or maybe even just a little?

STEP 4 Choose one or two of your favourite solutions – they don't have to be perfect, in fact most of the time solutions are not perfect, they're just OK.

STEP 5 Plan how and when you will try them out.

STEP 6 Try them. Did they work?

STEP 7 If not, try some other ones.

STEP 8 Stop and remind yourself that it's great you have remembered to practise solving problems, no matter what the outcome.

Let's see these steps in action:

Lin was really into art and drama, and often thought that she would like to work in theatre or the film industry. You might remember from an earlier chapter that Lin's parents had other plans for her and they thought she needed to study hard and go to university. She thought they probably wanted her to be a doctor, like her older sister. She did know that they wanted her to do a 'proper' job.

Although Lin wanted to please her parents, she didn't have much interest in science or medicine. She couldn't really think of anything she wanted to do except drama or art. It was time to start looking at university courses and Lin had ordered a prospectus that included courses in drama, theatre and film. She worried about what her parents would think. She thought about keeping it a secret but knew that eventually they would find out.

This kept going round and round in her mind, and she was feeling really stuck and worried. Then she realized that this was a problem she needed to deal with because it was getting her down. She applied the steps of the problem-solving process.

253

STEP 1 My problem is that I don't want to do a course that my parents want me to do and in fact I want a different career to the one they want for me.

STEP 2 Possible solutions:

1. 'Just forget the course I want to do and go along with my parents' wishes.'
2. 'Forget the whole thing and run away.'
3. 'Apply to the drama course without telling my parents.'
4. 'Talk to my friend about this and see what her advice is.'
5. 'Tell my parents that I'm going to apply to both medicine and drama because I haven't made up my mind yet.'
6. 'Don't apply to any courses and become a circus performer instead.'
7. 'Talk to my parents and tell them I don't want to do medicine.'

STEP 3 How good is each solution?

1. 'This would be the easy option but the problem won't go away and I will still feel miserable and worried.'
2. 'This would definitely not solve the problem and I don't have anywhere to run away to, plus I don't have any money.'
3. 'I could do this but my parents will eventually find out and then I will have to face them anyway and they might be really angry with me for not saying anything.'
4. 'My friend is always good at giving advice, maybe she'll help me.'

5. 'This would be so scary and hard! My parents would probably try to talk me out of it. At least they would know that I'm not that interested in medicine.'
6. 'This is just a silly one, I don't even like the circus!'
7. 'This would be like number five above. So very, very hard but it would be the truth. Maybe they would get really annoyed, but maybe they wouldn't and maybe they would actually understand.'

STEP 4 My favourite solutions are number four and number five.

STEP 5 I'm going to talk to my friend first. I will call her on Friday after school. After this, depending on what advice she gives me, I'll try to talk to my parents over the weekend, when they are both really relaxed on Saturday evening.

STEP 6 I talked to my friend. She said that she had a similar problem with the courses she was applying for. We talked about it for ages and we both decided to be honest with our parents to see what they say. We promised to phone each other on Sunday to talk about how it went.

On Saturday evening, after dinner when my parents were quite relaxed, I sat down and told them about my problem. I said that I understood why they wanted me to do medicine but I explained that I had no interest in it.

They both listened and I showed them the prospectus for the courses I was interested in. My dad was cross and started to get angry. My mum helped him to calm down a bit and talk about it more. It was really scary but it was such a big relief for me to tell them how I really felt. They agreed to have a think about it and to read the prospectus. I agreed to also have a bit more of a think about other courses. We were due to visit some universities and they agreed to visit one of the ones that does drama.

STEP 7 No need for this one yet.

STEP 8 These solutions helped me feel better, even though the problem isn't completely sorted. I'm really pleased that I chose to face this problem head on and not to run away from it!

Do you remember Emily's problem from the previous chapter? Emily found out that some of her friends were hanging around with the people who were bullying her. She didn't know what to do about this and it was bothering her. Emily tried some problem solving to see if it would help her.

STEP 1 My problem is some of my friends are spending time with the bullies and I don't know what is going on and whether they like me.

STEP 2 Possible solutions:

1. Talk to these friends and find out what they think.
2. Forget the whole thing and just stay away from them and everyone.
3. Just spend time with the people who still want to be my friends.

STEP 3 How good is each solution?

1. This would be really hard and they might just tell me to go away. I would maybe find out why they were spending time with them.
2. I wouldn't find out what was going on but this would be easy to do.
3. This one would make me feel better.

STEP 4 My favourite solutions are numbers one and three.

STEP 5 I will spend time with my best friend and ask her if she will go over with me to our other friends and ask what they were doing with the bullies. It would be easier if we did it together.

STEP 6 My best friend and I spoke to our other friends. They said that they still wanted to be our friends some of the time but they also wanted to hang out with the other girls (the bullies) some of the time. They said that one of the other girls was going to have a karaoke party and they wanted to get invited to it. I got to find out what is going on and it doesn't sound like they hate me or anything.

STEPS 7 & 8 Doing problem solving wasn't as hard as I thought. It helped me to see that I don't think I want to be good friends with these girls any more because they only want to spend time with me and my best friend when it suits them. It might be better just to spend time with the people who really like me. With the other girls I'll be nice to them but I won't think of them as very good friends.

Your turn – have a practise at solving a problem

Think of a problem you are having in your life right now. It could be something really big, like having relationship difficulties with someone important, or being bullied, or getting into trouble at school or somewhere else. Or it could be something quite small, like forgetting where you put your favourite shoes, or not being able to do your chores. Or your problem might fit somewhere in the middle, not huge, but not so little either.

STEP 1 Name it:

The problem is

_____

_____

_____

STEP 2 Come up with some possible solutions – go on, add some funny and ridiculous ones too, it helps with imagination.

_____

_____

_____

_____

_____

_____

STEP 3 Have a think about each solution and how good you think it is – will it solve the problem completely or maybe even just a little?

_____

_____

_____

_____

_____

_____

_____

STEP 4 Choose one or two of your favourite solutions – they don't have to be perfect, in fact most of the time solutions are not perfect, they're just OK.

My favourite solutions are

_____

_____

_____

_____

_____

STEP 5 Plan how and when you will try them out.

_____

_____

_____

_____

_____

_____

STEP 6 Try them. Did it work?

_____

_____

_____

_____

_____

STEP 7 If not, try some other ones – which ones will you try next? Do you need to think of some extra solutions?

_____

_____

_____

_____

_____

_____

STEP 8 Stop and remind yourself that it's great you have remembered to practise solving problems, no matter what the outcome.

How do you feel now?

_____

_____

_____

_____

_____

_____

This technique can be used for any problems that come up. After a while it becomes easier to use it quickly. Sometimes you will discover that solving the problem on your own is impossible and then one of your solutions might be about getting others to help you.

In fact, this might then become another problem to be solved.

'My problem is that I need help with my problem and I don't know who the best person or people are to help me with this'.

There might be lots of different solutions you can come up with for this particular problem. As you practise problem solving more your confidence will go up. Your mood will also improve once you feel you are doing something about your problems.

Caution: Some very BIG life problems definitely need the help of others (for example, parents separating) so do think about who could help if you are experiencing very big problems. Don't suffer alone.

Could you think of a problem to work on? No 'problem' if you can't think of anything right now. That's OK. You can always use this worksheet later when you come across a problem that you want to solve.

TAKE-HOME MESSAGES

Problems happen to everyone and often they help us to learn important things about ourselves, others and the way the world works. Learning how to solve problems, and practising problem solving regularly helps us to feel more in control and builds our confidence.

Part 4

Other things to try

12

Additional tools

Most of the strategies we have discussed so far are based on CBT principles and we know from many studies that CBT is helpful for people with depression. There are other techniques and ideas that can be very helpful for depression too but these haven't been studied yet in the same way as CBT. That's not to say that these additional ideas don't work! We just don't know enough about them yet to be really sure. Hopefully new studies in the near future can tell us more about what is most effective and for whom.

So the following suggestions, although not directly based on lots of research evidence, might be worth trying as some people find these very helpful.

Relaxation

You may remember that being very stressed is a bit like adding fuel to the depression 'fire', so it makes sense to find ways to be more relaxed. One of the best ways to be more relaxed is to do more things that you like and that you value. You learned

all about that in Chapter 8. Some people like to have additional strategies for relaxing and some people use these at night in bed. There are two good relaxation methods that seem to work for a lot of people:

Slow breathing into your tummy

Put one of your hands on your tummy and breathe slowly through your nose so that your tummy fills with air and you can see or feel your hand rising. Then breathe slowly out. Do this for a few minutes. After a while you will work out the speed of breathing that works best for you. This type of breathing tells your body that 'everything is OK and calm' and your body responds by relaxing. Try to use this technique at different times of the day until you get really good at it.

Tensing and relaxing your muscles

• Start at the top of your body and tense the muscles in your face and neck (pretend you have just eaten something disgusting and screw up your face as much as possible). Hold this for a few seconds and then let go. Can you feel the difference in how your face muscles feel?

• Then move down to your shoulders – bring them up towards your head and scrunch them up as much as possible. Then let go and enjoy the relaxed feeling in your shoulder muscles.

• Now it's your arms. Clench your fists and tense your arms, as if you were a robot. Hold, then let go.

• Then work on your back and stomach. Bring your stomach in as much as possible and tense the muscles in your back. Hold, then let go.

• You're probably getting good at this now.

• Now your bottom. Pretend you are trying to make your bottom look as small as possible and tighten all the muscles. Hold, then let go.

• Finally, do the same with your legs and feet.

How does your body feel now? It's best to start practising this when you are feeling pretty relaxed anyway. After a bit of practice you will get really good at using this strategy whenever you need it.

Improving your relationships and being assertive

You may remember that when people are depressed they often find being with other people and getting along more difficult. They often cut themselves off from people and prefer to be alone. This is understandable but it keeps depression going. It is important to put thought and time into the relationships that matter to you. This might be very hard at first because you won't feel like it (see **fake it till you make it** pp. 290–1).

Who do I know that I used to like spending time with?

_____

_____

_____

_____

_____

Who matters to me?

_____

_____

_____

_____

_____

Once you identify the people who are important then it's time to work out how you are going to put more effort and time into these relationships.

My ideas for improving my relationships (e.g. arrange to meet these people, call them up, send them a text, chat through the computer, buy them a tiny present like a chocolate bar, invite them over to my house, ask them how they are, help them with a problem or a chore, just hang out together, etc.).

_____

_____

_____

_____

_____

Another thing that helps people with their relationships is remembering to be assertive. This means standing up for yourself, respecting your own opinions and wishes and telling others what you want in a confident way. Being assertive does not mean telling others what to do or being really pushy or angry. Being assertive helps to build strong relationships with people because it's a way of letting others know who you really are, and your true feelings and opinions. If you always keep your opinions and feelings hidden from others, or if you only push them on to others through anger then they don't get a chance to get to know you properly.

Robert got really angry with his mate, Neil, at school a few times because Neil was now going out with Robert's ex-girlfriend, Chloe. Robert didn't think Neil even liked her that much and he couldn't understand why they were together. One time this led to Robert punching Neil in the stomach. This was making Robert feel isolated and low. He used to like hanging around with Neil but now he was so angry. Robert decided to apologize to Neil for hitting him. He contacted him on Facebook. Neil suggested they go riding on their bikes the next day. Robert told Neil that he was angry about him going out with Chloe. He also told Neil that it made it difficult for him to hang out with him because he didn't want to run into Chloe. Neil said he understood and he told Robert that he really, really liked Chloe and wanted to keep seeing her. Robert was a bit surprised to hear this and he told Neil that this was OK since he didn't think they would ever get back together again. They agreed that it would be good to meet up again, without Chloe around.

Is there anything that's OK?

When things are not going well and when we feel terrible, it's hard to see anything in our lives that feels right. One of the ways that depression makes us slide downwards is by making everything look bad so that we are unable to notice any of the good or OK bits, even if they are there.

Do you remember the sections earlier about breaking out of the low mood swamp and not getting stuck in thinking traps? The following method can be another way that sometimes helps people to get out of the traps. And it's about noticing things that are OK. You're probably thinking, 'Really? That seems a bit simple,' or you might be thinking, 'Nothing is OK.' It might seem simple but it can be incredibly helpful if you do it regularly. So here is how it goes:

Have a think about everything and everyone who is in your life right now. Is there anything that's not too bad? For example, do you have a warm, comfortable house to live in? Is one of your teachers at school nice? Do you have any friends who you think are OK? Are you generally healthy? Do you own anything that you quite like, such as a bike, a phone, an MP3 player, a computer or a TV? Are you able to eat food that you like? Is there a person in your family who you love and who loves you back? Do you have a pet that you care about? Is there one thing about school that you think is OK? Are there people or ideas that can help you when you are feeling very low? Can you go for a walk or exercise in some way if you choose to?

There are hundreds of things to consider in your life and we suggest you stop and think about them in this section. There is space below to jot some of these down. You might be able to think of more as you go about your day and notice things that are OK. Depression causes people to notice all the things that are not OK. In fact, often it makes OK things look as though they're not. You can start to reverse this process by making yourself notice things that are OK. Once you start to notice things that are OK, you will start to naturally see more and more things that are positive in your life.

Things that are OK

Things about where I live (e.g. I like the fact my house is close to a corner shop, my house is nice overall, I like my garden, etc.)

Things about my school (e.g. I quite like one of my subjects and the teacher is OK, our uniform is not too bad, etc.)

Things about the people in my family (e.g. My mum is good to talk to sometimes, I like seeing my cousins, etc.)

Things I own (e.g. I love my phone, my trainers are quite cool, etc.)

Things about people or animals I care about (e.g. My dog is so funny sometimes, my sister is OK most of the time, etc.)

Things about my health and body (e.g. I am pretty healthy overall, I think my hair is OK, I'm pretty strong, etc.)

Things about my freedom to do things if I choose (e.g. I can go out and see friends if I want to, I could join a club or sport team if I wanted to, etc.)

Things about my comfort (e.g. I have a nice bedroom, the food I eat is OK, etc.)

Things about my country (e.g. Most people have freedom in my country, I like the fact that my country supports lots of different sports, etc.)

Tiny little things (e.g. I have some cool clothes, I got a text from my friend the other day, etc.)

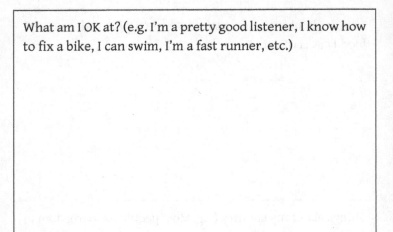

What am I OK at? (e.g. I'm a pretty good listener, I know how to fix a bike, I can swim, I'm a fast runner, etc.)

Being a bit nicer to myself

When people are depressed, usually one of the things that they become very good at is being negative about themselves. Some people refer to this as 'beating yourself up' or 'expecting yourself to be perfect'.

Imagine for a moment that you are watching a football game in the park. The game is being played by two teams of children. They're all about seven or eight years old. Their parents are looking on, shouting and cheering. You spot a boy who looks quite shy and he's trying to get into the game but he's finding it hard to get the ball. Every time he gets near the ball it gets passed to someone else. All of a sudden, one of the boys passes the ball to him and this shy boy has a go at getting a goal. The ball misses the goal by only a couple of feet.

Imagine that the coach starts telling this boy that he's no good, that he's letting the team down, that he can't do anything right and that he may as well not be in the team. Will this make him feel good? Will this motivate him to keep playing? Will he have another go at getting a goal? No, it's not likely. This is not a good way to encourage someone or to build their confidence.

What would you say to this boy if you were the coach and you could give him a pep talk at half time? You might say 'well done for trying', 'that was a good shot', 'keep doing what you're doing', 'it was so close', 'you're bound to get one in soon' or 'you're doing so much better as the game goes on'. You might even give him an encouraging pat on the back. You can probably see that giving the boy lots of praise and encouragement will make him feel good and will motivate him to keep playing his best. He might even score in the second half.

We talk to ourselves all the time (very often just in our heads rather than out loud). We can choose to talk to ourselves like the first coach or like the second coach. Depression makes you more likely to be negative towards yourself and to put yourself down so you need to make an extra effort to remember to be your own encouraging coach. This is particularly important when you're trying things out for the first time or when you're having a go at doing things to help your mood. Being nice to yourself and giving yourself praise and encouragement will help you to feel better and will motivate you to keep trying new solutions and ideas. Scolding yourself or telling yourself that you are no good will have the same effect as it did on the shy boy.

Many people with depression find this idea very difficult. That's fine if you do too. Just be aware of this for now and if you are able to give yourself some encouragement from time to time rather than telling yourself off then that is a fantastic start. Some people find it helpful to actually give themselves rewards for little things that they try. Rewards are another way of telling yourself 'well done' and giving yourself encouragement. They don't have to be big or expensive.

Lin decided to reward herself every time she chose to be active rather than staying in her room. It was easy to decide on her first reward, a piece of chocolate. Then she made a list of other rewards she would like (e.g. new sketchbook, time on the computer looking at art supplies, an app for her phone, watching her favourite film, a cup cake tray).

Lin showed the list to her mum and explained how the rewards will help her to be more active. Lin's mum thought this was a good idea and she helped Lin come up with a few other rewards, especially for doing chores around the house. Some of Lin's rewards also helped her to be more active so it was like a double positive effect on her mood.

It might be a good idea to get some help with rewards and this is something worth talking to your parents about. Why don't you show them this section of the book and see if they can come up with some rewards with you? It's important to remember that the rewards don't have to cost a lot of money, and lots of rewards are almost free. For example, some people find it really rewarding when their parents give them lots of encouragement, especially when they are doing something they find difficult. It can also be very rewarding to receive praise from others when overcoming a problem. If you like you can talk to your parents about how you would like to be encouraged and praised by them. You can also talk to your friends or relatives and see if they have any ideas.

It's also important to include rewards you can do on your own. Reward yourself for trying new things or difficult things even if you don't succeed. This can include saying positive things to yourself (don't worry it can be in your head, you don't need to speak out loud). Think of the kind of encouraging and positive things a coach would say to you and say them to yourself – here are some examples, you can probably think of many more:

- 'Well done, that was really hard but I had a good go at it.'
- 'Let's have another go and see how I get on.'
- 'That was really good.'
- 'Close one, maybe next time I'll manage it.'
- 'Well done for trying.'
- 'Great try, really good.'

My ideas for rewards when I need some encouragement:

1. _____

2. _____

3. _____

4. _____

5. _____

Being more in the here and now

This idea is pretty special. There are lots of studies looking at this and how it can help people with depression. Being more in the **here and now** simply means focusing on what's in front of you rather than what has already happened or what is going to happen in the future. Sometimes this is referred to as mindfulness. We mentioned it as a good way to deal with stuck thoughts in Chapter 9.

The reason mindfulness is a useful technique is that often when we are feeling low or anxious we are **not** in the **here and now**. Rather we are more **up in our head**, thinking over and over again about past events – things that didn't work out, things people said or did, things that seem unfair or things we think we failed at. Or we might be thinking over and over about future events – things that might go wrong, things we have to do, things people might say to us or things we won't be good at.

Our thoughts go around and around and around and around and around and... around and...

So being more in the **here and now** gives our negative thinking a bit of a break. And when we reduce negative thinking we also reduce how low or worried we feel.

283

It's a bit like riding a bike

Being in the **here and now** could be compared with riding a bike. To ride a bike well and safely you need to focus on what is in front of you on the road at the time. It would be pretty hard to focus if you spent your whole time thinking about what just happened a few minutes or hours ago. Imagine trying to ride well if you are constantly thinking about how long the last traffic lights took to turn green, or the guy who swerved in front of you half an hour ago, or the bumps in the road at the last junction. You might actually miss what's in front of you.

It would be the same if you spent the whole time thinking about what is ahead of you. So you might be riding along and be thinking all the time about what the next road will be like, whether there will be any turns in the road and what sort of speed you will go at when you get there. Hopefully you can see that this sort of thinking would also mean that you might completely miss what is right there in front of you at the time. Now, when riding a bike this might actually be dangerous as you could miss a car driving out on to the road or you might go through a red light.

In everyday life always thinking about the past or the future is, of course, much less dangerous than when riding a bike, but it can also have negative consequences. It means you are always replaying things that have already happened and are gone, or you are predicting things that haven't even happened and may never happen, things that might be around the corner (but might not be!). This can lead to low mood and anxiety. In any case, you miss out on what is right there in front of you, at that very moment.

Try this out for yourself. Spend five to fifteen minutes of your day focusing on what is right there in front of you. It helps when you start to actually describe the scene to yourself. So you might say something like:

'I'm sitting in the garden, it is quite warm, I can feel the wind against my face, the seat I'm sitting on is hard, I can hear a couple of birds and someone mowing the lawn, I can smell the grass a little, it's quite bright outside, I can taste the orange juice I just drank, the garden looks dry and a bit yellow, I can see a line of ants on the ground.'

Your mind will then go **whoosh!** into the past or the future. This is **natural** as our minds do this all the time. When it does this just come back into the **here and now** and describe a few more things. It takes lots of practice and the most important thing is not to think you are doing it wrong or to judge yourself. Just have a go, even if it's only for one minute. If you practise it will become much easier. It may help you to feel better and you may notice things that you otherwise would have missed if you were 'up in your head'. You can do this almost anywhere, no matter what you are doing. You could practise being in the **here and now** when walking, or when doing the dishes, or when sitting on the bus.

Accepting feelings and events

Many of us feel stuck in our lives. We might be experiencing events that are hard, stressful and painful. People may be behaving in ways that we don't like and we may be feeling things that we would rather not. The strategy we are going to introduce here is a little opposite to what we were suggesting earlier in Chapters 9 and 11. This strategy is about accepting things as they are.

We suggest that you try the earlier strategies first and see whether changing the way you think about things helps you to feel better and to act differently. Also, have a go at problem solving the difficulties in your life. It's important to give these strategies a good go. You might find that they make a difference for some things but no difference at all for other things. Some things can be dealt with and changed by us but we may not be able to change everything. Some thoughts can be challenged and changed but some kinds of thoughts can get stuck.

When we are faced with difficult situations and feelings it is easy to become frustrated and angry with how things are. We may feel that things are **not fair**, and we may wish for things or people to be different. The problem is that sometimes it is difficult to change the way things are, or it might take a while for things to change. It's also very hard to change how others behave. Meanwhile, we are left feeling frustrated and stressed about the situation. Frustration and stress are certainly good fuel for the depression 'fire': the more you pile on, the bigger the feeling of depression will get. So while it is understandable to feel frustrated and stressed when things are tough, it actually ends up making you feel worse. The worse you feel, the more things will look bad.

It is useful to try another way. Accepting things the way they are for a while can give us a bit of a **holiday** from our feelings of frustration and stress. It's a way of saying 'OK, I've tried to think differently and I've tried to problem solve this. Now I'm going to try and accept the way things are for a while as well. It might not change what is actually happening, but it might make me feel more relaxed. And I know that the more relaxed I am, the better my mood is.' So, in other words, I'm not changing the situation but I'm changing how I'm reacting to it.

It's a bit like trying to get rid of an unwanted guest at a party

See the video here: www.youtube.com/watch?v=VYht-guymF4

The more you try to get rid of the guest, the more frustrated and unhappy you become when they refuse to leave. Also, you miss out on all the good things that are happening at your party and you miss out on spending time with your friends. Accepting that the guest is going to stay helps you to feel calmer and to focus on the things that matter. You might also notice that the guest is not as bad as you first thought.

This can be a big shift because rather than **fighting** with or against the situation, you are deciding to just **let it be**, almost as if you removed yourself to the side a bit. It allows you to describe what is happening and notice how it makes you feel, but it doesn't pull you into thoughts such as 'it's not fair', 'why is this happening to me?', 'why can't things be different?', 'why can't they act differently?', 'it shouldn't be this way'. If you read Chapter 9 then you will remember that our thoughts and feelings are very closely linked. So you can imagine that these types of thoughts are going to make you feel . . . yep, much worse!

Accepting certain things as they are does not mean you are giving up or giving in, or wanting things to stay this way. It does mean that you can find calmer ways of thinking, relax more and perhaps become more interested in the things that make you feel better and those things that have meaning and value in your life.

Note: If someone is causing you harm in any way then this is a situation that you must NOT accept. You need to tell someone you trust about it and get help immediately.

If you are having problems with bullying then tell your parents or teacher straight away. Bullying is NOT OK and you will need help and support from others.

Find more advice on bullying here:

www.bullying.co.uk/general-advice

Emily often wished that the girls who used to bully her would like her and that she was accepted into their group. She thought it was so unfair that they didn't want to be friends with her. She kept thinking about why this was happening to her and why those girls just didn't change their attitude. This made her feel really low and left out. She tried to come up with lots of different ideas about how to get them to like her. She even tried some of them but none of them worked. Emily found that thoughts about how unfair it was kept on coming up for her and making her miserable . . . She tried challenging her thoughts by using some of the ideas in Chapter 9. This worked for a while but then her frustrated and angry feelings kept coming back every time she saw the girls at school or thought about them. Emily finally saw that her need for things to be different with these girls was actually making her feel worse. She saw that for now there was nothing much she could do about it. The school knew that these girls bullied her sometimes and she knew she could go and talk to her teacher at any time about it. So Emily decided to **accept** the fact that these girls didn't want to be her friends. This wasn't easy at first. She had to keep reminding herself that:

'That's the way things are right now and I will put my mind to other things that are important to me.'

This definitely helped a bit. Accepting things as they are helped Emily to feel less miserable and frustrated about a situation that she couldn't change. Emily still sometimes wished things were different but she was much less upset about it. And this meant that she thought about it less and was able to enjoy her time more with the friends who did like her.

Acting 'as if' – fake it till you make it

You might be wondering what we mean by this title. Some people refer to the saying 'fake it till you make it' when they talk about trying to cope in a new job, for example, when not feeling particularly confident in the beginning. It involves acting confident until you actually do start to feel confident with more and more experience. It can help with motivating a person to take on tasks and challenges that would otherwise seem too daunting.

This approach can also be applied to helping yourself feel better and less depressed. In the beginning when people try to break out of the depression swamp it can be really hard. We have encouraged you in Chapter 4 to activate yourself and to do more of the things you used to enjoy. This is much easier said than done. Most of the time when people are low they do not feel like doing anything. So we encourage you to 'fake it till you make it'.

This involves **acting as if you are feeling better** (before you actually do feel better). So think to yourself, how would I be right now if I was feeling better? What would I be doing? Who would I be talking to? What would my body posture look like? What would I be wearing? How would my face look? Create this image of yourself in your mind and decide on an activity. Now go and act as if you are feeling this way and do the activity. We are basically asking you to be an actor, a bit like if you were doing a role in a play or a show or film on TV. Go on, act it out for half an hour or so. We know it won't feel real, we know it will feel fake to begin with.

Notice how the activity makes you feel. Were you faking it all the way through or were there moments when you didn't have to pretend? Was there anything about this activity that is worth repeating? When you do this a few times sometimes something quite cool starts to happen. People find that they are no longer faking it as much as before. They sometimes actually start to feel better, without pretending that they are feeling better. This idea can be used for many different situations. It is all about getting back into the habit of doing things you used to do when you were not depressed. So go on, fake it till you make it. What have you got to lose by trying it?

Being you and being OK with this

This is a tough one! You might be feeling lots of different pressures from friends, people at school, and people in magazines and on TV to be a certain way.

This is OK if it makes you feel OK. So you might like to wear similar clothes to your friends or you may all share similar opinions or interests. You might also like to do similar things to your friends or people at school and you may like the idea of 'fitting in'. But if wanting to be like others starts to make you feel not OK on a regular basis then maybe this is adding to your depression. If you think this is the case then perhaps it is time to try a different approach to how you see yourself and how much you compare yourself with others.

The other thing is that we are exposed to images on TV and in magazines all the time, and sometimes this can make us feel like we should be the same as the people and images in the media. This might be about how we look, how much we weigh, what clothes and shoes we wear, what phone we have, where we go, what we do, who we spend time with . . . aaaaaaagh!

No one can ever keep up with the people we see in the media. Why not? Because often the things we see in the media are not entirely based on real life. Often only the best bits of a whole situation are shown so we don't really get the full picture.

It's the same on social media sites. People don't show us the full picture, only the bits they want us to see. If spending time using social media is making you feel worse, we suggest you reduce the time or stop completely for a few days. You could ask your parents to help with this.

So, for example, we might see and read about a celebrity who has a fantastic body, perfect hair, a fantastic boyfriend, goes to the coolest parties, hangs out with the coolest people and seems to be happy all the time. What we don't see is that perhaps that same celebrity woke up with a face full of acne and frizzy hair that morning, had a huge argument with her boyfriend, spent the whole day in her stained jogging bottoms and was upset because she hadn't been invited to a big celebrity party that night. On a day like that, the celebrity might find that she needs to **act as if she is feeling better** (see above!). Faking it can work for anyone for some of the time.

The point is that we just don't know what is really going on with others, we only really know about our closest friends and relatives. So while things may seem really great for others, and this makes people want to be just like other people, the best option is to just be yourself.

So how can I be myself and be OK with this? For some people this is pretty easy, they just naturally seem to be able to like who they are. Sometimes they might 'fake it' for a short time, just to get over a tricky situation, but most of the time they are able to be true to who they are. For many other people this is much harder and requires practice and more practice. Try the following:

1. Remind yourself regularly that everyone is an individual and there are no two people who are alike on this entire planet. This is a good thing!
2. Give yourself permission regularly to have your own opinions.
3. If you catch yourself comparing yourself with others, remember that you probably don't have the full picture of that person's life.
4. As often as you can, do things that you like doing rather than things you feel you **should** be doing.
5. Write down a list of things that are all about you (e.g. I like horses, I can't stand mustard, I want to work outdoors someday, I really don't like jogging, my favourite thing in my wardrobe is my green T-shirt, pop music is definitely not for me, etc.).
6. Look at this list regularly and add/change things as you feel like it.

7. Write a list of your dreams and goals for the future (allow yourself to write anything you like, big or small).

8. Remind yourself about your values and goals.

9. Remind yourself regularly that your likes, dislikes, opinions and dreams are all about you and this is OK.

10. Hang out with people who make you feel good and who encourage you to be you.

11. Pick one thing you like about yourself each day and think back to it all day long (e.g. I like that I'm tall, I like my toes, my nose is not too bad, I like that I can draw, I'm alright at sport, I'm quite caring, etc.).

TAKE-HOME MESSAGES

Different strategies and ideas work for different people and it's a good idea to have a go at some of these to see if it can help you feel better too. Whatever you have decided to work on, it's important to give it a good chance to work by practising regularly and keeping going with it for at least a few weeks.

Part 5

Keeping it going

13

Planning for the future and finding more help

Beating depression is rarely a completely straight road. There are usually twists and turns, bumps in the road, unexpected hurdles, and hills that go up and down. Sometimes things will seem to go well and you will feel like you are making progress, and at other times it will feel like you are not making any progress at all and it might even feel like you're going backwards for a while.

This is natural.

The most important thing to remember is to keep going and to keep using the strategies that you have learnt in this book. Hopefully you have already made some progress by using some or most of our suggestions. Some people, as they work on overcoming their depression, also find there are other strategies and things that work for them that are not in this book. They sometimes spot things that are very personal to them that seem to make a positive difference. Perhaps you have noticed some extra things that work for you?

All things change all the time, it is the way this world works. While this is unsettling in some situations, because sometimes we want things to stay the same, it is good news when it comes to low mood and depression. That's because we know it's possible for the depression and terrible feelings to change too.

In this chapter we encourage you to **note down any strategies that have helped you to feel better** and **plan how to keep using these.** We also encourage you to **plan how to spot the warning signs early on** to reduce the chances of depression coming back or getting worse in the future.

Things that have helped me

Understanding what depression is ☐

Understanding my symptoms ☐

Understanding where my depression came from ☐

Understanding what keeps my depression going ☐

Setting goals ☐

Hearing about other teenagers' experiences ☐

Knowing that lots of other people feel like I do ☐

Putting together an emergency toolkit ☐

Knowing who to speak with about my thoughts and feelings ☐

Talking to my GP about how I feel ☐

Talking to my parents/teacher/other responsible adults ☐

Finding out about how to look after myself (e.g. food, exercise) ☐

Knowing how to tackle sleep problems ☐

Getting more information and facts about depression ☐

Understanding the CBT links and how CBT works ☐

Understanding about how activity helps ☐

Being more active and doing things I used to enjoy ☐

Regularly reviewing my goals ☐

Understanding that how I think is closely related to how I feel ☐

Changing the way I think about things ☐

Setting up fact finders and putting things to the test ☐

Solving problems more often ☐

Using relaxation strategies ☐

Improving my relationships and being more assertive ☐

Noticing things that are OK ☐

Being a bit nicer to myself ☐

Being more in the here and now ☐

Accepting things that can't be changed for now ☐

Acting as if I feel better ☐

Being more OK with being me ☐

Looking up websites or contacting other organizations for more information and help ☐

Other things I have noticed, situations and strategies that seem to work for me:

_____

_____

_____

_____

_____

_____

Things that are better, the same, worse

What is my score on the **Short Mood and Feelings Questionnaire** (see pp. 12–14) now?

Total score _____

How does that compare with my earlier scores?

Look back at your original goals at the beginning of the book. How much progress have you made in relation to these goals? Maybe it's time to set some new goals?

Goal 1 _____ Progress   0 1 2 3 4 5 6 7 8 9 10
(0 = no progress at all, 10 = I've totally reached my goal)

Goal 2 _____ Progress   0 1 2 3 4 5 6 7 8 9 10
(0 = no progress at all, 10 = I've totally reached my goal)

Goal 3 _____ Progress   0 1 2 3 4 5 6 7 8 9 10
(0 = no progress at all, 10 = I've totally reached my goal)

Things/symptoms that seem to be better:

_____

_____

_____

_____

_____

Things/symptoms that have pretty much stayed the same:

_____

_____

_____

_____

_____

Things/symptoms that have got worse:

_____

_____

_____

_____

_____

My new goals

1. _____

2. _____

3. _____

4. _____

How will I remember to keep using the helpful strategies?

This is the really tricky part, especially if things are going a bit better. As things improve it is easy to forget to keep practising and using the strategies that have helped because it feels like there is less need for them. This sometimes also applies to times when things seem to be a bit worse because you might think 'what's the point?' In this case this is usually the depression talking.

The message is the same for both of the situations above:

Keep practising and **using** the **strategies.**

The more you practise and use the strategies, the better you will feel, and the easier it will become to use them. Applying the strategies will become a good habit that you just automatically follow, without too much effort.

If you know how to ride a bike you may be able to relate to this. In the beginning when you're learning it is really hard. With practice it becomes much easier, but you still have to concentrate pretty hard on not falling off and not running into anything. After a lot of practice it just becomes automatic. You can ride a bike without falling off without much effort and when unexpected things come up, like for example when you need to turn suddenly to avoid a tree stump, you can do this pretty well. It's the same with anything new that we are learning.

This is also the aim with the strategies for dealing with depression – to make all the helpful responses become second nature to you. This is so that when things come up and the stress possibly gets worse, you will automatically deal with things in a helpful way and decrease the chances of experiencing low mood again.

A good way of reminding yourself to keep using the strategies is to have a list of things that work for you somewhere to hand. Some people keep it in their wallet, others save it in their phone, or you could put up Post-it Notes in different places in your room or places where you are sure to see them. Another good idea is to set aside about half an hour each week to think about how things are going and to make any plans for how to keep the progress moving in the right direction. It's a good plan to pick the same time each week, at a time that is usually free. Many people need help with remembering to do this so it's a good idea to involve others, such as your parents, to help you with this task.

I will remind myself to keep using the helpful strategies by:

Making a list of helpful strategies and putting the list somewhere visible	☐
I will put this list (e.g. on the fridge, on my desk in my room, in my wallet)	
Making time each week to think about my progress and plan how to keep it going	☐
My chosen day and time for this is:	
I can think of other ways to remind myself and these are:	
Asking others to help me remember	☐
The people I will ask to help me are:	

What are my warning signs?

It's a good idea to get to know your warning signs. What we mean is those early signs and symptoms that could indicate depression or low mood may be around the corner. For some people this may be when they are going through a stressful time. For others it could be when relationships are not going well or when they notice they have stopped doing things they enjoy. The warning signs will be very different for each person. Below are some suggestions based on what others have told us over the years. There is also a space for you to write down your own warning signs. If you review your progress regularly you can also use this time to note down any warning signs that you have noticed.

I've noticed I've stopped exercising and it's something I usually enjoy ☐

I'm not getting along well with people in my life ☐

Things are pretty stressful right now ☐

I've noticed I'm spending too much time alone ☐

I'm eating a lot of junk food and this is unusual ☐

I've been a bit more sensitive and tearful lately ☐

I've noticed I'm avoiding things that I usually get on with ☐

My sleep pattern has changed ☐

I'm cancelling things and staying away from people more ☐

I'm not spending much time on my hobbies and things I enjoy ☐

I'm feeling really irritable ☐

I'm not spending much time doing relaxing things ☐

I can't be bothered to eat/everything tastes like cardboard ☐

I'm really tired and unmotivated ☐

If I had the choice I would just stay in bed ☐

I'm getting really stressed about little things ☐

I'm feeling more anxious in general ☐

I'm arguing with my family/others a lot ☐

There are stressful things coming up soon (e.g. exams) ☐

My own warning signs that are not listed above:

_____

_____

_____

_____

_____

_____

_____

What is my plan when I notice the warning signs?

By now we're pretty sure you know the answer to this! That's right, when you spot the warning signs it is time to firstly think about whether you need extra support and secondly to use the strategies that have helped you before. It is not a good idea to struggle with things alone and hope that they will improve by themselves. It is much better to involve others, ask for help, use the strategies that help and make a plan for how you will keep depression away.

I'm OK, I just need to put together a plan for how to reduce the stress ☐

I think I need to use the strategies that helped more often ☐

I think I need a bit of extra support ☐

I'm really struggling, I definitely need an emergency plan and much more support ☐

The people I will talk to are:

_____

_____

_____

I definitely need to go back to all the helpful strategies ☐

My other notes and ideas:

_____

_____

_____

_____

_____

_____

_____

_____

_____

_____

_____

_____

_____

_____

_____

TAKE-HOME MESSAGES

Overcoming depression can have ups and downs. Some days it will feel like you are making progress and other days you may feel the opposite. This is all part of the journey and it might be helpful if you remind yourself about this regularly, particularly on those less good days. If you continue to practise the strategies in this book there is a really good chance that your depression will get much better. Being on the lookout for things that you know make you feel worse will help you to take action in time, and prevent depression from coming back.

We wish you all the very best on your journey.

Good luck!

Appendix 1:

Summary of useful places to find more info and help

Information about depression and CBT

National Institute of Clinical Excellence (NICE) – information about depression in young people and evidence-based treatment.

www.nice.org.uk/CG28

Young Minds – information, advice, support and helplines for young people affected by mental health problems, and their parents.

www.youngminds.org.uk

Parents' helpline: 0808 802 5544 (Monday–Friday, 9.30 a.m.–4 p.m.)

www.youngminds.org.uk/for_parents

Royal College of Psychiatrists – information for young people and parents about mental health and a range of related topics. www.rcpsych.ac.uk/healthadvice/parentsandyouthinfo.aspx

www.rcpsych.ac.uk/expertadvice.aspx

www.rcpsych.ac.uk/healthadvice/parentsandyouthinfo/ youngpeople/cbt.aspx

British Association for Behavioural and Cognitive Psychotherapies (BABCP) – organization providing information about CBT and accreditation of CBT therapists.

www.babcp.com/public/what-is-cbt.aspx

NHS Choices

Information from the National Health Service on conditions, treatments, local services and healthy living.

www.nhs.uk/conditions/cognitive-behavioural-therapy/ pages/Introduction.aspx

Further information, support and advice

Depression Alliance – national charity providing information and articles about depression.

www.depressionalliance.org

Rethink – information and helpline for anyone affected by mental health problems.

Helpline: 0300 5000 927 (Monday–Friday, 10 a.m.–2 p.m.)

www.rethink.org

Mental Health Foundation – information about mental health and related issues.

www.mentalhealth.org.uk

Mind – information on mental health problems and treatments.

www.mind.org.uk

Helpline: 0300 123 3393 (Monday–Friday, 9 a.m.–6 p.m.)

Youth Space – information and advice about a range of issues affecting young people, including mental health problems.

www.youthspace.me/help_and_advice/471_depression

Cruse – support and helpline for bereaved people and those caring for bereaved people.

Helpline: 0844 477 9400 (Monday–Friday, 9.30 a.m.–5 p.m. and until 8 p.m. Tuesday–Thursday)

www.cruse.org.uk

Health Talk Online – information and patient experiences for various health and mental health problems (includes separate section for young people)

www.healthtalkonline.org/young-peoples-experiences/ depression-and-low-mood/topics

MindFull – provides information and online counselling and support for young people.

www.mindful.org

Respect Yourself – daily messages for young people, which focus on your strengths and the future.

www.respectyourself.org.uk

Crisis support and information

ChildLine – free confidential twenty-four-hour helpline or online chat service for young people up to nineteen years of age.

Helpline: 0800 1111 (24 hours)

www.childline.org.uk

Samaritans – free confidential twenty-four-hour helpline for anyone needing support.

Helpline: 08457 90 90 90 (24 hours)

www.samaritans.org

Papyrus HOPELineUK – free confidential helpline or online support for anyone having suicidal thoughts, or for anyone concerned about a young person at risk of harming themselves.

Helpline: 0800 068 4141 (Monday–Friday, 10 a.m.–10 p.m.; Saturday–Sunday, 2 p.m.–5 p.m.)

www.papyrus-uk.org/support/for-you

Harmless – support for people who self-harm, and support for the families and friends of those who self-harm.

www.harmless.org.uk

Social Services – support for young people and families affected by a range of difficulties or for anyone concerned about the welfare of a young person. Find your nearest service via your council website or in the local directory.

NSPCC – information and helplines for anyone concerned about a young person.

Helpline: 0808 800 5000 (24 hours)

www.nspcc.org.uk

Adfam – support and advice for families affected by drugs and alcohol.

www.adfam.org.uk

FRANK – confidential information and advice about drugs, offering online chat as well as a texting service.

Helpline: 0300 123 6600 (24 hours)

www.talktofrank.com

Drinkline – confidential information, help and advice for anyone affected by alcohol.

Helpline: 0300 123 1110 (Monday–Friday, 9 a.m.–8 p.m.; Saturday–Sunday, 11 a.m.–4 p.m.)

www.patient.co.uk/support/drinkline

Alcohol Concern – information about the harmful effects of alcohol.

www.alcoholconcern.org.uk

Bullying UK – advice and support for anyone affected by bullying.

Helpline: 0808 800 2222 (every day, 7 a.m.–midnight; calls diverted to the Samaritans at other times)

www.bullying.co.uk

Further self-help resources

NHS – self-help and information about exercise for depression.

www.nhs.uk/Conditions/stress-anxiety-depression/Pages/exercise-for-depression.aspx

Moodgym – web-based CBT programme.

www.moodgym.anu.edu.au

Students Against Depression – information, support and self-help ideas.

www.studentsagainstdepression.org

www.studentsagainstdepression.org/understand-depression/why-me-why-now

Moodjuice – self-help booklet for people experiencing depression.

www.moodjuice.scot.nhs.uk/depression.asp

Living Life to the Full – range of booklets, worksheets and computer-based self-help modules.

www.livinglifetothefull.com

GET Self Help – free worksheets and CBT tools.

www.getselfhelp.co.uk/freedownloads2.htm

Mindfulness and compassion

Be Mindful – information about how mindfulness can reduce depression, anxiety and stress.

www.bemindful.co.uk

Mindful Youth – information about mindfulness for young people.

www.mindfulyouth.org

The Compassionate Mind Foundation – promoting wellbeing through compassion.

www.compassionatemind.co.uk

Books

N. Dummett & C. Williams, *Overcoming Teenage Low Mood and Depression: A Five Areas Approach* (London: Hodder Arnold, 2008).

P. Gilbert, *Overcoming Depression: A Self-Help Guide Using Cognitive Behavioral Techniques* (London: Constable & Robinson, 2009).

K. Mears & M. Freeston, *Overcoming Worry: A Self-Help Guide Using Cognitive Behavioral Techniques* (London: Constable & Robinson, 2008).

L. Seiler, *Cool Connections with Cognitive Behavioural Therapy: Encouraging Self-Esteem, Resilience and Well-Being in Children and Young People Using CBT Approaches* (London: Jessica Kingsley Publishers, 2008).

Appendix 2:

How to find a therapist

There are a few different ways to get a bit of extra help with some of the ideas in this book. You might find that your family and your friends are supportive and encouraging and we have suggested getting their help if you can.

There are also places you can get help by telephone, text or email, and again we have suggested several of these throughout the book and in Appendix 1.

You might prefer to get some extra help from a real person, outside the family. This is where a therapist might be relevant to you.

There are many different kinds of therapy. This can be confusing, but only some forms of therapy are recommended for depression in young people. These are CBT (which is what this book is based on), family therapy, interpersonal therapy and psychodynamic psychotherapy. Your therapist should be able to explain what each form of therapy is about and how it can help.

What should I expect if I see a therapist?

Most people don't know what goes on in therapy; after all, therapy usually happens behind closed doors. We think it's important to know what to expect. This can help you get the best out of therapy. Here are some questions that lots of people ask and worry about.

What do I have to talk about?

Seeing a therapist, especially at the start, can be very nerve-wracking. Don't worry if you can't think what to say or don't know where to start. Your therapist will be used to people being nervous and they will do everything possible to help you feel more at ease. If it is helpful you can ask a parent, carer or friend to come with you to therapy sessions. If you do not want this to happen you should tell your therapist and usually this is absolutely fine.

Will the therapist keep things private?

Your therapist will talk to you about confidentiality. Normally everything you tell them will be kept private but there may be times when this is not possible. Your therapist will explain when they would not be able to keep your discussions private.

Why does my therapist want to record our sessions?

Many CBT therapists will record your therapy sessions on video or audio. They use the recordings in supervision. Supervision is where their work is checked. This means that they are able to work effectively and safely. Your therapist will explain this to you and ask for permission to record the session. You don't have to agree but it is very helpful if you do. It helps make sure that you and everybody else gets the best possible help.

How will my therapist treat me?

When you start therapy you start a new relationship with a person you didn't know before. Your therapist should listen to you, accept you as a person, be warm and empathic, and understand your point of view. The bond or relationship you develop with your therapist is a very important part of having CBT or any other therapy. Trust is an important part of your relationship. Your therapist should be open with you at all times. They should tell you what therapy will involve, how long it will take, and how it will work.

It's important to feel respected by your therapist and to feel 'heard'. Your therapist is going to be older than you and will have quite a lot of training and experience. They have expertise in being a therapist. This can make it hard for you to feel like you can be real partners, but you have more experience than they do about your life, about what it is like to be you, and about what you want in the future. So you each bring your own expertise and this is the partnership. You will have lots of ways to take part and even to lead the therapy.

What will I have to do?

Therapy is about working together. That's right – you and your therapist are partners. CBT, in particular, is about **collaboration**. This means that you decide together what you are going to try to change, you agree how to try to change, and you both take responsibility for what you do.

You know what **you** want to be different. Your CBT therapist will help you identify those goals in your first few sessions. It's important that you are able to play a full part in therapy. At the beginning of each session you and your therapist will agree on the agenda for this session. This means that you decide what you will do during the session and what is most important.

We've used the word 'work' to describe what happens in therapy. This is because therapy is not something that is done to you. It is something you take part in and put effort into. That's how real change happens – there really aren't any shortcuts.

What's this about homework?

In CBT, you and your therapist will develop *assignments* for you to do between sessions. We think assignments are a better word to use than 'homework'. This is because you and your therapist set assignments together. These are important because they help you change in the real world, outside of therapy. Therapy only lasts for an hour a week and will come to an end. Assignments help you to bridge the space between therapy sessions. They will also help you to learn and practise new skills and new ways of behaving and thinking.

A lot of CBT assignments will look like the exercises in this book. If you don't want to do an assignment or feel it is wrong tell your therapist – don't forget you are partners and collaborators. You can help decide on something else that suits you better.

What if my therapist asks me to do something I don't want to?

Sometimes when you have therapy you discover that you have to face your fears in order to overcome them. This can be very, very difficult and frightening. Your therapist should be able to explain why it is important and it's important that you understand this. But it will not make it any easier. The trust you have in your therapist and the strength of your relationship will help you face your fears. You will not be asked to do anything against your will but you may decide that you do have to do things you find very difficult. Your therapist will help you or your parents to find and use different kinds of support.

How long will therapy last?

There are different stages of therapy. In CBT your therapist will explain how long therapy is likely to last (how many sessions over how many weeks). You will review this from time to time to see if it needs to change. The number of therapy sessions you have is hard to predict. It's unlikely that you would have more than twenty sessions. Each session will last about an hour.

During the first few sessions you and your therapist get to know each other and build trust and confidence. Your therapist will want to find out about you – about important things in your life and in your past, and about your strengths and weaknesses, and your hopes and dreams. You will identify your goals – what it is that you want to change. Your therapist is likely to ask you to fill in some questionnaires. These give them more information about your difficulties. Together you will build an understanding of your problems. This is called a **formulation**. The formulation is like a story of your life so far. It will include things that might have caused your problems or made them worse, and things that keep them going.

In the middle part of therapy you will work together to tackle your difficulties. You will focus on changing the things that keep your problems going. Most likely these will be your behaviours (like avoiding things) or your thoughts. You will try out different ways to think and to behave. You will have assignments between sessions and will build on these at each session. You and your therapist will monitor how you are doing and change your plans depending on how things go. You may go a bit faster, or a bit slower than expected. You might add some goals and take away other ones.

Therapy will end. The final stage of therapy prepares you to move on and live the rest of your life. It's important to see therapy as a stepping stone to prepare you for your best possible future.

Where can I find a therapist?

Usually the best place to start is with your GP. If you live in the UK he or she can refer you to specialist mental health services for young people. Some specialist services let you refer yourself without going to your GP but this is different in different parts of the country. If you search the Internet for 'Child and Adolescent Mental Health Services' in your nearest town or city you will find where they are and if they take direct referrals.

You might also have counselling services at your school or college that you can use without going to the GP.

Finally, some therapists work privately. This means that you have to pay them for their help. Your GP is probably the best person to talk to about this but you can also find private therapists by contacting specific organizations (e.g. BABCP, British Psychological Association, your insurance company if you have health insurance).

What do I need to know about my therapist?

Finding a therapist is not very difficult but there are a few things to keep in mind to make sure you get the help you need. It can be good to involve your parent(s) in finding a therapist.

There are a lot of different kinds of people who offer therapy.

Psychotherapists, therapists and counsellors

Anyone can call themselves a 'therapist' or a 'psychotherapist' or a 'counsellor', even after a two-day training course, so it's important to ask them questions about their training. A good therapist will be pleased that you asked them and will give you as much information as you want.

The information in this book is based on a form of psychological therapy known as CBT – Cognitive Behaviour Therapy. In the UK and many other countries face-to-face CBT is recommended for young people who have depression. If your depression is mild, self-help CBT, like we use in this book, is recommended.

If you want to work with a therapist using the same ideas as we have talked about in this book you should ask to be referred for CBT. Your therapist should have had special training in CBT and should also have regular supervision to make sure that their work is as good as it can be.

Some CBT therapists are nurses, occupational therapists, social workers or some other kind of professional. They will have done an extra one-year course to train in CBT. After this, if they have the right kind of experience and supervision, they can register as a CBT therapist with the British Association of Behavioural and Cognitive Psychotherapy (BABCP). If they are registered (accredited) with the BABCP, you can look them up on the BABCP website – www.babcp.org.

If your therapist is accredited by the BABCP they have to have regular supervision, keep up to date with the research, and have regular updates to their training. Their registration is renewed every five years. If they do anything wrong they can be 'struck off' the register. If you are offered CBT by a therapist who is not a psychologist you should make sure that they are accredited by the BABCP.

Clinical and counselling psychologists

In the UK nobody is allowed to call themselves a 'clinical psychologist' or a 'counselling psychologist' unless they are registered and listed on the Health and Care Professions Council. These titles are protected by law. You can check that they are registered by going to the HCPC website and searching for their name – www.hcpc-uk.org. Anyone at all can say they are a 'psychologist'. Be aware, they do not have to be registered and may not have the right training.

All registered clinical and counselling psychologists have completed an undergraduate degree in psychology and post-graduate training, which is usually for three years. This is usually a 'doctorate' degree so most clinical and counselling psychologists will have the title 'Doctor'. Psychologists are regulated by the HCPC and they have to stick to rules and regulations about the best and safest ways to practise.

Psychologists often specialize in different types of therapy, including CBT. But not all psychologists offer CBT or have special training, so it is important to ask them. They may offer family therapy or interpersonal therapy for depression and these are also recommended for young people. The best way to find out if they offer CBT is to ask them. Some psychologists are also accredited with the BABCP but it is not required for them to practise CBT.

Other professionals

If you are referred to the NHS for help with depression you might meet other kinds of professionals. For example, if you are prescribed anti-depressant medication this will be by a psychiatrist. A psychiatrist is a medical doctor who specializes in mental health. They will see you to review how you are getting on and to alter your medication, if necessary.

You might also be seen by a nurse or a primary care mental health worker. They may be able to support you using CBT techniques but they cannot offer you CBT unless they have had specialist training and supervision. They may be trained in other effective therapies such as family therapy or interpersonal therapy. Feel free to ask, all good therapists are happy to discuss their training and experience.

Appendix 3:

Quick view of the book chapters and topics

Some people find it difficult to read much and especially when they are feeling low it can be really hard to focus. This section provides a summary of the main things discussed in the book so that if you can't read much you can have a quick look and see if anything catches your eye. You might see something in this list that seems worth trying and then if you want to find out more you can go straight to that section and find it easily. Or maybe you can just show the section to someone you trust and they can help you with this.

Part 1 – Is this book for me?

Chapter 1 – What is depression and what can be done about it? (p. 3)

- Find out what to expect from this book.
- Find out what depression is.
- Discover if you have depression.
- Check your symptoms.

- How to talk to your GP.
- Find out where to get more help.
- Meet three teenagers with depression – p. 20.

Chapter 2 – Goals (p. 31)

- Find out why having goals is important for getting better – if you don't know where you're heading, you won't know which roads to take to get there!
- Learn how to set goals and decide on your own goals.

Part 2 – Looking after yourself

Chapter 3 – Dealing with difficult thoughts and unhelpful or risky behaviours (p. 45)

- This chapter is for you if you are having thoughts about death, suicide or wanting to harm yourself. This chapter is also for you if you already self-harm.
- Find out what to do when you have these types of thoughts.
- Put together an emergency toolkit to keep you safe.
- Learn more helpful ways to deal with urges to self-harm.
- Find out where to get more help.
- Learn about drugs and alcohol and how to get more support.

Chapter 4 – Looking after yourself – the basics (p. 67)

- Learn the facts about sleep and how to deal with sleeping problems.
- Find out about the effect of food on mood and how to eat well.

- Discover the facts about exercise and how it could help you feel better.

Part 3 – Getting started

Chapter 5 – Why me? (p. 107)

- This chapter is for you if you are wondering why some people get depressed.
- Learn about the main causes of depression – biology, life events/triggers and how we cope.
- Have a go at figuring out where your depression came from.

Chapter 6 – The CBT idea (p. 124)

- Find out about a treatment for depression called Cognitive Behaviour Therapy (CBT).
- Discover how thoughts, feelings and behaviours are linked and what this means.
- See examples of how CBT works.

Chapter 7 – I want to make more sense of my depression (p. 135)

- Learn how certain things keep depression going.
- Discover more about how your depression started and what is keeping it going now.
- Start getting some clues about what could make it go away.

Chapter 8 – Feeling and doing (p. 151)

- Find out why we do less and less when feeling depressed.
- Learn how doing less makes us feel worse.
- Ideas for how to start doing more to beat depression – activity logs.
- Have a think about your life values.

Chapter 9 – Thoughts on trial (p. 188)

- Find out more about how certain thoughts can make us feel worse.
- Discover how we can see things in different ways.
- Learn how to catch thoughts.
- Are you getting stuck in thinking traps?
- Find out how to challenge thoughts that make you depressed and find more helpful ways of thinking.

Chapter 10 – Testing things out – getting the facts (p. 227)

- Find out how to put thoughts to the test by using fact finders.
- Discover examples of fact finders and design your own.

Chapter 11 – Solving problems (p. 247)

- This chapter is for anyone who has ever had problems – everyone!
- Find ways of dealing with problems to help you feel more confident and in control.
- See problem solving in action.

Part 4 – Other things to try

Chapter 12 – Additional tools (p. 267)

- This section provides additional tools, strategies and ideas for beating depression. It won't be for everyone, but you might find something really useful that you like.
- I want to relax more! Here you can find two useful relaxation strategies.
- This section is all about improving your relationships with the people who count and being more assertive.
- Is there anything that's OK? Being on the lookout for things that are OK.
- Being nicer to myself. Treating yourself with kindness and giving yourself praise and encouragement.
- Being more in the here and now. Using mindfulness to feel better.
- Accepting feelings and events. Allowing things to be as they are in order to reduce distress.
- Acting as if you feel better – fake it till you make it. A way of motivating yourself to do the things you would rather avoid.
- Being you and being OK with this. Appreciating your individuality.

Part 5 – Keeping it going

Chapter 13 – Planning for the future and finding more help (p. 297)

- Identifying all the things that have helped your depression.
- Planning how to keep using the helpful strategies.

- Learning how to detect warning signs that depression could be returning.
- Planning what to do if you spot warning signs.
- For more information and help, see Appendix 1.

Appendix 4:

Extra copies of worksheets

My goals

So firstly, what would you like to be different? (This can be a depression symptom you would like to get rid of or it could be something else that you would like to be different in your life, or it could be something you have stopped doing because of the depression that you would like to start again.)

_____

_____

_____

_____

You might say things like 'to feel happier', 'to feel less lonely', 'to be less angry', 'to be me again', 'to not cry all the time', 'to feel less stressed', 'to have more fun', 'to be less tired', 'to get along with my parents more', 'to see my friends more'.

This is a very good start.

So let's say that this change happened. What would this be like?

_____

_____

_____

And what would you be doing that perhaps you are not doing at the moment?

_____

_____

_____

Who would be there?

_____

_____

_____

How would you be feeling?

_____

_____

_____

Would you be seeing anyone more often?

_____

_____

_____

What else would be happening in your everyday life?

_____

_____

_____

Who would notice this change?

_____

_____

_____

What would they notice that was different about you?

_____

_____

_____

Now let's think a bit more long term.

Two years from now. How old will you be in two years? Imagine for a moment that you have been able to travel forward in time to this point.

How would you like to see yourself in this future? What would you like to be doing? Where is this? Who would be there? What would be happening around you? How would you feel? What else would be going on?

_____

_____

_____

_____

What about **five years from now**? Right, transport yourself there now. How old are you in five years' time?

What would you like to see? What does an older, more positive you look like? What are you wearing? What are you doing? Where is this? Who is there? What is happening around you? How do you feel? What else is going on?

_____

_____

_____

_____

My emergency toolkit

1. Who can I talk to about my thoughts?

_____

2. List of people and/or organizations I can contact when I'm feeling very bad:

_____

_____

_____

_____

MyGP'sphonenumber_____

3. Things to look out for and avoid because they seem to make my mood and thoughts much worse (triggers):

_____

_____

_____

_____

_____

4. List of things that will help to distract me when I'm feeling very bad:

_____

_____

_____

_____

_____

_____

5. My helpful strategies for dealing with self-harming or risky behaviours:

_____

_____

_____

_____

_____

_____

My sleep diary

Complete the diary every day. It's probably best to do it first thing in the morning

	Day 1	Day 2	Day 3	Day 4	Day 5	Day 6	Day 7
What time did you go to bed?							
How long did it take you to go to sleep?							
How many times did you wake up in the night?							
After falling asleep how long were you awake for during the night?							
At what time did you wake up (the last time)?							
What time did you get up and out of bed?							
How long in total did you spend in bed?							
How well did you sleep (1 = very bad, 5 = very good)							

My hot cross bun examples:

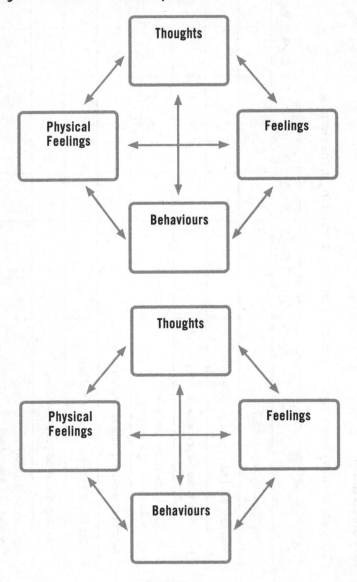

My life values

What is important to you about each of these areas?

Me	Things that matter	People that matter
Hobbies/fun	Education and work	Family
Keeping healthy	Things I need to do	Friends
Looking after myself	The bigger picture	Boyfriend/girlfriend

My activity list

Physical activity	Do now?	Used to do?
Swimming		
Playing sport (e.g. tennis, football)		
Dancing		
Other physical activity (e.g. riding, running, cycling)		
Skills/work/education	**Do now?**	**Used to do?**
Learning to drive		
Paid work (e.g. babysitting, paper round)		
School		
Homework		
Music lesson		
Creative things	**Do now?**	**Used to do?**
Drama		
Art (e.g. painting, drawing, sculpture)		
Playing music		
Cooking		
Writing (e.g. stories, diary, poetry)		

Extra copies of worksheets

Being sociable/relationships	Do now?	Used to do?
Watching TV with family		
Having a family meal		
Shopping with friends		
Voluntary work		
Spending time with family and friends		
Having fun	**Do now?**	**Used to do?**
Going to the cinema		
Playing computer games		
Going to a party		
Having friends to stay overnight		
Planning a party or social event		

My activity log – today's date _____

Date, time	Activity – what I did, with whom and where	Achievement	Closeness	Enjoyment	Important?
7 a.m.–8 a.m.					
8 a.m.–9 a.m.					
9 a.m.–10 a.m.					
10 a.m.–11 a.m.					
11 a.m.–12 noon					
12 noon–1 p.m.					
1 p.m.–2 p.m.					
2 p.m.–3 p.m.					
3 p.m.–4 p.m.					
4 p.m.–5 p.m.					
5 p.m.–6 p.m.					

6 p.m.–7 p.m.	7 p.m.–8 p.m.	8 p.m.–9 p.m.	9 p.m.–10 p.m.	10 p.m.–11 p.m.	11 p.m.–12 midnight	12 midnight–1 a.m.	1 a.m.–2 a.m.	2 a.m.–3 a.m.	3 a.m.–4 a.m.	4 a.m.–5 a.m.	5 a.m.–6 a.m.	7 a.m.–8 a.m.

My life values

This is what I did (from the activity log) to match my values

Me	Things that matter	People that matter
Hobbies/fun	Education and work	Family
Keeping healthy	Things I need to do	Friends
Looking after myself	The bigger picture	Boyfriend/girlfriend

My thought-catching log

Time and date	Situation – what happened	What you thought How much you believe it	Feeling How strong is the feeling?

My thought-challenging ideas

Situation _____

Thought	Feeling How strong? 0–100 per cent	New, more helpful thought	Feeling How strong? 0–100 per cent

My fact finder

Thought(s) to test
Fact finder
Prediction
Do it

So what happened?

Was the prediction right?

What does it all mean?

Is there a balanced view?

What's next?

What next?

Problem solving

STEP 1 Name it:

The problem is

_____

_____

_____

_____

_____

STEP 2 Come up with some possible solutions – go on, add some funny and ridiculous ones too, it helps with imagination.

_____

_____

_____

_____

_____

STEP 3 Have a think about each solution and how good you think it is – will it solve the problem completely or maybe even just a little?

_____

_____

_____

_____

_____

_____

STEP 4 Choose one or two of your favourite solutions – they don't have to be perfect, in fact most of the time solutions are not perfect, they're just OK.

My favourite solutions are

_____

_____

_____

_____

_____

STEP 5 Plan how and when you will try them out.

_____

_____

_____

_____

_____

_____

STEP 6 Try them. Did it work?

_____

_____

_____

_____

_____

_____

_____

STEP 7 If not, try some other ones – which ones will you try next? Do you need to think of some extra solutions?

_____

_____

_____

_____

_____

_____

STEP 8 Stop and remind yourself that it's great you have remembered to practise solving problems, no matter what the outcome.

How do you feel now?

_____

_____

_____

_____

_____

_____

Things that are OK

Things about where I live (e.g. I like the fact my house is close to a corner shop, my house is nice overall, I like my garden, etc.)

Things about my school (e.g. I quite like one of my subjects and the teacher is OK, our uniform is not too bad, etc.)

Things about the people in my family (e.g. My mum is good to talk to sometimes, I like seeing my cousins, etc.)

Things I own (e.g. I love my phone, my trainers are quite cool, etc.)

Things about people or animals I care about (e.g. My dog is so funny sometimes, my sister is OK most of the time, etc.)

Things about my health and body (e.g. I am pretty healthy overall, I think my hair is OK, I'm pretty strong, etc.)

Things about my freedom to do things if I choose (e.g. I can go out and see friends if I want to, I could join a club or sport team if I wanted to, etc.)

Things about my comfort (e.g. I have a nice bedroom, the food I eat is OK, etc.)

Things about my country (e.g. Most people have freedom in my country, I like the fact that my country supports lots of different sports, etc.)

Tiny little things (e.g. I have some cool clothes, I got a text from my friend the other day, etc.)

What am I OK at? (e.g. I'm a pretty good listener, I know how to fix a bike, I can swim, I'm a fast runner, etc.)

Index

A

accepting things/ events 285–8
acting OK 290–1, 292
activity 151, 156
  activity list 157–8
  activity log 151, 152,
    166–76
  attention to life values
    152–5, 176–83
  avoidance 161
  getting started 184–5
  inactivity and depression
    159–63, 187
  keeping going 185–7
  starting place for
    overcoming depression
    164–5
  starting small 184, 186
  see also exercise
Adfam website 65

A&E (accident and emergency
  department) 50
alcohol and drugs 59, 63–5,
  76–7, 89
Alcohol Concern website 65
alone, being 26, 69, 158–9, 162
anti-depressants 15–16
appearance, personal 69
appetite loss 99
  see also eating habits
assertiveness, importance of
  271
avoidance behaviour 161

B

BABCP 134
bad influences, people who are
  55, 59, 63
balance, life 117
balanced views 229–30

'beating yourself up,' stop
    278–80
bed, your 85–6
    see also sleeping problems
behaviour experiments *see* fact
    finders for balanced views
behavioural changes 69–74
biases, thinking 196–9
biological causes of depression
    113–15
black and white thinking trap
    209
brains, human 98
breakfast, importance of 98
breathing techniques 268
brooding on things 220–1
bullying 29, 288

cigarettes 89
Cognitive Behavioural Therapy
    (CBT) 17, 124–33, 226, 267
    interpretations of events
        128–30
    low mood swamp - sliding
        down *v.* breaking out
        131–2
    see also activity; problem
        solving; thoughts,
        managing your
compassion for self 223
confidence 250
cooking 102
coping strategies (dealing with
    urges to self-harm) 57–9
cycles, vicious 69–74

C

caffeine 85, 89
calculator, symptoms 7
challenging your thoughts
    211–15
Child and Adolescent Mental
    Health Services (CAMHS)
    16
ChildLine 47
chocolate 89

D

delaying self-harm 57
depression
    biological influences 113–
        15, 136
    causes of 108–15, 136–7
    defined 5–6, 107–8
    inactivity and 159–60
    is there a quick fix? 138
    life events 111–12, 136

making sense of your own
118–23, 135–9, 148–50
medication 15–16
practising helpful strategies
303–5
recording positive results
299–303
resilience to 116–18
Short Mood and Feelings
Questionnaire 11–13,
301
symptoms of 7–9
trigger events 109–10, 136
warning signs 306–9
what keeps it going? 137–8
see also activity; Cognitive
Behavioural Therapy
(CBT); self-harming
(and thoughts about);
thoughts, managing
your
diet *see* eating habits
distractions from negative
thoughts 51, 57–8, 221–2
doctors *see* GPs (general
practitioners)
drinking habits, healthy 98
Drinkline 65
drugs and alcohol 59, 63–5, 76–7

dwelling on things 162–3,
220–5, 251

E

eating habits 76–7
depression and appetite
98–9
developing healthy 99–102
food and emotional
wellbeing 97
guidelines for healthy
100–2
junk food 98, 99, 101–2
emergency toolkit 48–51, 60,
61–2
encouragement, self 280–2
exercise 58, 76–7, 86
different attitudes to 91–6
do you dislike or hate
exercise? 92–4
do you still exercise? 91
have you stopped enjoying?
91–2
health benefits 89–90
starting small 96–7
see also activity
experiences of depression
Emily 27–9, 34, 70–1, 99,

121, 146–7, 201–2, 233,
242–4, 256–8, 289
Lin 24–6, 33, 71, 81, 88–9, 99,
120, 143–5, 154, 171–6,
178–81, 232, 237–41,
253–4, 280–2
Robert 21–3, 32, 46, 52–4,
68–9, 80, 87, 91–2,
99, 119, 127–30, 133,
139–42, 159, 161, 231,
234–7, 272–3

F

fact finders for balanced views
227–30
examples 233–44
setting up 230–3
your own 244–6
'fake it till you make it' 290–1,
292
family
genetic links to depression
113–15, 136
support 14, 35, 47, 84, 88,
101, 102, 117, 153, 185,
224, 244
food *see* eating habits
FRANK 65

friends 35, 59, 78, 101, 153, 185
bad influences 55, 59, 63

G

genetic links to depression
113–15, 136
goals 31–5
ideas for 39–40
working out your 35–9
GPs (general practitioners)
anti-depressants 16
drugs and alcohol abuse 65
exercise and mood 90
mindfulness groups 224–5
sleeping problems 89
thoughts of self-harming/
suicide 47, 49
what to tell your 14–15, 47

H

harming yourself *see* self-
harming (and thoughts
about)
Harmless 60
health, looking after your 67–8
developing healthy habits
75–7

different attitudes to
    exercise 91–7
exercise benefits 89–90
resetting your internal
    clock 83–9
vicious cycles 69–74
    see also activity; eating
        habits; sleeping
        problems
helplines 47
here and now, living in the
    282–5

I

inactivity and depression
    159–62, 187
    see also activity; exercise
internal clock 79–89

J

jumping to conclusions 210–11
junk food 98, 99

L

life events, stressful 111–12

M

media influences 291–2
medication for depression
    15–16
meditation 224–5
memories 197, 223
mind reading 210
mindful charity 103
mindfulness 224–5, 283–5

N

negative thoughts *see* 'beating
    yourself up,' stop;
    depression; thoughts,
    managing your;
    thoughts of self-
    harming/ suicide
NHS (National Health Service)
    99, 103, 134

O

on-call psychiatrists 50
optimism 118
over-generalizing 209

P

Papyrus HOPELine UK 47
parents, support from your
14, 35, 47, 84, 88, 101,
102, 117, 185, 224,
244
people to avoid 55, 59, 63
pessimism 118
physical symptoms 71, 125
positive reinforcement 162
positive thoughts 273–8
see also here and now,
living in the; problem
solving; thoughts,
managing your
practising helpful strategies
303–5
predictions, negative 210
problem solving 222
ask 'how?' not 'why?' 251
different perceptions
of problems 248–51
problems and life 247–8
step by step 252–62
when to get help 263
progress, recording positive
298–303

Q

Questionnaire, Short Mood and
Feelings 11–13, 301

R

relationships, improving 270–3
relaxation techniques 267–9
resilience to depression 116–18
rewarding yourself 280
risky behaviour 59, 63–4
Royal College of Psychiatrists
134
rumination/ 'stuck thoughts'
162–3, 220–5, 251

S

Samaritans 47
school
dislike of physical
education 92, 94
sleeping patterns 78
see also experiences of
depression
self-blame 210, 223
self-harming (and thoughts
about) 45–7

avoiding people who
encourage 55
dealing with 54–9
delaying 57
distractions from 51, 57–8
emergency toolkit 48–51,
60, 61–2
helplines 47–8
questions to ask yourself
55–6
safer methods 58–9
stopping 55–9
triggers 50–1
urges will pass 59–60
sex, unsafe 59
Short Mood and Feelings
Questionnaire (SMFQ)
12–13
sleeping problems 76–9, 89
keeping a sleep diary
81–3
out of sync internal clock
79–83
resetting your internal
clock 83–9
slow breathing 268
smoking 89
social media 55, 292
social support 117

solving problems *see* problem
solving
sports *see* activity; exercise
stopping self-harming 55–6
stuck thoughts 162–3, 220–5,
251
Students Against Depression
103, 123
suicidal thoughts 14, 45–7
distractions from 51
emergency toolkit 48–51,
60, 61–2
helplines 47–8
triggers 50–1
support groups/ helplines 47–8
symptoms of depression 7–9

T

teachers 14, 47
tensing and relaxing muscles
269
thoughts, managing your 188
catching negative thoughts
203–8
challenging your thoughts
211–15
finding more helpful
thoughts 216–19

how they make us feel bad
192–3
how we make sense of the
world 194–9
'letting go' of negative
thoughts 222–3
living in the 'here and now'
282–3
nature of thoughts 189–91
rumination/ 'stuck
thoughts' 162–3, 220–5
sneaky negative thoughts
199
snowballing negative
thoughts 199–200
thinking biases 196–9
thinking traps 199–211, 273–4
thought catching log 207–8
see also problem solving
thoughts of self-harming/
suicide 45–7
distractions from 51
emergency toolkit 48–51,
60, 61–2
helplines 47–8
triggers 50–1
see also self-harming (and
thoughts about);
suicidal thoughts

tiredness *see* sleeping problems
toolkit for bad times,
emergency 48–51, 60,
61–2
traps, thinking 199–211, 273–8
triggers events, depression
109–10
triggers, negative thought 50–1

V

values, life 152–5, 176–83
vicious cycles 69–74, 151
see also thoughts, managing
your

W

warning signs
plans to act on 308–9
recognizing 306–7
weekend sleep patterns 87
weight gain 76
worry time, allocating 224

Y

yourself, being OK being 291–4
Youth Space 123, 226